THE INDOOR GARDEN SECRET

HOW TO GROW FOOD 365 DAYS A YEAR

SUSAN PATTERSON, MASTER GARDENER

BACKYARD
· VITALITY ·

CONTENTS

If words are seeds,
let flowers grow
from your mouth,
not weeds.
If hearts are gardens,
plant those flowers
in the chest of the ones
who exist around you.

— *R.H. Swaney*

Yes, You Can Garden 365 Days a Year

Imagine sitting down on a cold winter's day to a delicious and hearty meal prepared using fresh, homegrown vegetables. Imagine being able to pluck fragrant herbs from your windowsill and leafy greens for your favorite salads without ever having to step outdoors. Imagine having the most beautiful and healthy edible plants ever. Indoors... all year long. Is it possible, you might ask? The answer is a resounding yes, yes, yes!

I have been growing flowers and food for over thirty years and have experimented with all sorts of growing systems, from raised beds to hydroponics. One of my greatest passions is helping people realize just how easy it is to have access to safe and healthy food all year long - no matter where you live or how much space you have.

The benefits of gardening are far-reaching and include emotional, mental, and physical payoffs. There is no single person who would not gain something by adopting this popular pursuit.

Perhaps you have a vision in your mind of what it looks like to garden. Maybe you see someone hunched over with a hoe in hand, baking in the hot sun, with sweat dripping from their brow- working acres and acres of land in a grueling and never-ending cycle. Or, maybe your understanding of gardening comes from personal experience where you have labored hard with minimal results. I want to help erase any vision of back-breaking and brow-beating work that you have in your mind and replace it with something novel and exciting. Something that anyone can do!

Conjure up an image of yourself preparing an evening meal and reaching into your windowsill for a handful of fresh thyme, rosemary, or parsley—slicing spring onions and steaming kale picked just a few feet from your kitchen counter. No hot sun, no sweat, no acres and acres of land to work - only a few steps, and you have fresh and delicious homegrown food for you and your family. Does this sound like something that might interest you?

Growing food indoors 365 days of the year opens up a world of possibilities for anyone who desires to live a healthy life and reap the benefits of gardening.

After writing numerous best-selling gardening books including, *The Secret Garden, The Backyard Harvest, The Instant Box Garden Miracle, The Hydroponic Garden Secret,* and *Mastering Microgreens*, I thought it was time for a book dedicated entirely to growing indoor edible plants.

There is a green revolution of sorts happening now, as more and more people embrace growing food for excellent reasons. My motive for writing this book is to make gardening as accessible as possible - even to those who don't have any outdoor space. This book provides everything necessary to start growing your favorite fruit, veggies, and herbs right away, no matter where you live.

The Indoor Garden Secret is a perfect book for anyone interested in having easy access to a safe and healthy food supply all year long. It doesn't matter whether you live in a temperate climate or an area that sees more rain and snow than sunshine. It doesn't matter if you live on twenty acres or the twentieth floor of an apartment complex - you **CAN** be successful. You **CAN** enjoy healthy food without breaking your back or your bank.

As a **Certified Health Coach** and **Master Gardener**, I cannot stress enough that the time has come to embrace the gardening movement and take control of your health and food safety. Let me show you how to become a successful indoor gardener, no matter your skill level. Anyone can do this!

Everything that you need to know to enjoy a bountiful harvest inside the walls of your home is found right here in this book. I have even included a few of my favorite ways to use what you grow for health and wellness and some fun projects that will make the experience even more exciting.

There is no better time than right now to begin your indoor garden journey. Are you ready?

Happy growing.

Susan Patterson, CBHC, Master Gardener, and Author

> ## "The love of gardening is a seed once sown that never dies."
> ### - Gertrude Jekyll

A Special Thank You

I want to thank my creative husband Thomas who is always ready and willing to take on any gardening project with me, no matter how big or small!

GREAT REASONS TO GROW FOOD

While growing and preserving food is still a widespread activity in many cultures worldwide, it isn't necessarily popular in America. Many people take food for granted, merely going to the grocery store without much thought about where the produce originated. We just expect it to be there, right?

Imagine a world where grocery stores did not exist, where there would be no fresh veggies, fruits, or herbs unless you grew them yourself. While you may think this could never happen, I urge you to consider the reality. We are living in fragile times — times that require us to prepare for the possibility of a severe food shortage, or, at the very least, an increase in food recalls involving tainted fresh food on the grocery store shelves.

Here are some excellent reasons to grow food at home starting now!

You will save money

One of the factors that inspired me to start growing food was that it would save money. Organic produce can be expensive, but a pack of organic seeds? Not so bad.

Even with the cost of water and plants factored in, you can save quite a bit of money when you grow food instead of paying the high price at the grocery store. For example, a bag of organic baby spinach costs around $4 at the local grocery store, and it's only enough for a few servings.

Compare that to organic seeds, which are a fraction of the cost and yield about **six pounds of fresh spinach**. To me, it makes excellent sense. And even if you do have to work a little for it, you can still enjoy fresh, organic spinach all season long.

You will be healthier

Even more important than the savings is the opportunity to produce and consume nutrient-rich fruits, veggies, and herbs. Food that's grown organically, without synthetic pesticides, contains measurably more nutrients than non-organic foods.

In an analysis of over 300 studies published in 2014 in the *British Journal of Nutrition*, researchers found that organic crops, including everything from blueberries and apples to broccoli and carrots, had a substantially higher antioxidant concentration and other beneficial compounds. There were 50 percent more flavonols and anthocyanins in organic crops than conventional ones in just one example.

Plus, when you grow fruits and veggies, you tend to eat more of them. You also know more about what comes in contact with your food, and you control the harvest. Store-bought produce is often harvested too early and is lacking in essential nutrients.

You can protect your kids

When my kids were young, I remember being shocked when I read the staggering statistics about how susceptible young children are to pesticides. That was over twenty years ago, and unfortunately, things are even worse today.

According to the **National Academy of Sciences**, children are much more susceptible to chemicals than adults. Estimates show that 50% of lifetime pesticide exposure occurs during the first five years of life. The average child receives four times more exposure than an adult to at least eight widely used cancer-causing pesticides in food.
If nothing else convinces you, these discouraging statistics should encourage you to begin gardening for the health and safety of your children.

A food shortage won't impact you

During World War I, and especially World War II, Americans were asked to grow food to help support the war effort. Although we may not be in the middle of a world war, our food supply is exceptionally vulnerable nonetheless.

All you have to do is take a look around the world to see what might happen. In Venezuela, for example, citizens have been enduring a catastrophic food shortage due to an economic crisis and the total collapse of the food system that relied heavily on imported foods. As currency controls food imports, hyperinflation eats into salaries, and people have to line up for hours to buy basics like flour.

People are starving in that country. Amid the crisis, the government has advised Venezuelans to start growing edible crops and raising chickens. But gardening takes time, and if you don't know anything about it, it can take even longer.

Regardless of the type of government or those who are in power, any population that relies on imports for its food supply could be next on the list to experience a dire food shortage. The United States imports more food than any other nation on the planet, followed by China, Germany, Japan, and the United Kingdom.

There doesn't have to be a significant economic crisis, either. What happens if truck drivers go on strike or delivery trucks cannot deliver food to the stores? What if there is a fuel shortage that prevents them from delivering or causes the prices to skyrocket? Taking action now is a must to prevent future tragedies.

Your food will be fresh

Around one-fifth of the fresh vegetables in the United States come from overseas. How fresh can it be when it traveled thousands of miles to reach the grocery store shelf? The quality of store-bought produce gets lower and lower the further it has to travel. So unless you're buying from the farm or a local farmer's market, you're probably not getting the freshest foods.

However, when you grow your own, it doesn't get any fresher. You can choose when to harvest and consume what you produce when it reaches peak ripeness. It naturally tastes much better this way. Some have noted that before cultivating a home garden, they never really knew just how good a fresh tomato or perfectly ripe nectarine tasted.

You will be less stressed

There is something incredibly relaxing about spending time caring for plants, watching them bend and reach for the sun, and keeping an eye on them as they produce delicious food for your table.

Science even confirms how valuable growing a garden can be to your mental health. One study asked volunteers to perform a stressful activity followed by either 30 minutes of reading indoors or 30 minutes of gardening. While both managed to reduce stress, gardening had a much more dramatic impact. Many mental health experts and physicians have determined that getting out in the garden is excellent therapy. It is used to treat anxiety, depression, PTSD, and Alzheimer's disease, among many other ailments. Caring for plants, whether indoors or outdoors, is one of the best natural medicines around!

You'll help the planet

Our planet could use some love, and when you grow food, you'll be improving the earth and our environment in several ways. First, you won't be polluting the air by driving to the grocery store, and second, you'll be helping to cut back on the energy used by modern farming. Modern farming currently utilizes more petroleum than any other single industry! It consumes 12 percent of America's total energy supply. So if you grow your own, you're reducing pollution both from your travel and modern farm equipment.

Additional benefits of indoor gardening

If you have ever grown veggies, fruits, herbs, or flowers in containers, you know that it is a gratifying experience. Container gardening is a great way to bring plants closer to you for easier planting, care, and harvesting. It is the ultimate way to grow many plants in minimal space.

Container gardening is what allows you to have a thriving garden inside the walls of your home all year long. Contrary to popular belief, many plants, including fruits, vegetables, and herbs, are quite content to grow in containers. Here are just a few of the additional benefits of cultivating homegrown crops indoors.

- *Less risk of soil-borne diseases*
- *Less chance of insect infestation*
- *More control over soil, light, moisture, and temperature*
- *Easy to plant, care for, and harvest*
- *Beautify your home*
- *Easy to save seeds from heirloom plants*

GETTING TO KNOW
YOUR ZONES

When it comes to growing zones, you may be familiar with the
USDA or Sunset zones for growing outdoors. While the information
on these zones is useful when you plant in an outdoor garden, it
doesn't apply to indoor planting.

Believe it or not, your home has its very own growing zones. Indoor
growing zones provide the roadmap by which an indoor edible garden
can be successful.

Understanding these zones allow you to place your plants where they
will be the happiest and most productive.

Keep in mind that if you have very little or even zero natural light -
you can still grow edible crops with supplemental light from a grow
light system.

I suggest making a map of your indoor growing space and noting
where you have the best light options for the plants you wish to grow.

Bright light zones

Bright zones include south-facing rooms, spaces with east or west-facing windows, and below skylights. Spaces in these zones provide the most sunlight possible - especially in the spring and summer months. Be sure to keep your curtains open all the time to let in as much sunlight as possible.

- **Bright light grow zone #1** (BL1) - by a south-facing window-grow fruit, edible flowers, and herbs that love bright sunshine

- **Bright grow zone #2** (BL2) - by large west or east-facing windows - grow many herbs, edible flowers, small fruiting vegetables, and fruit crops like strawberries

- **Bright grow zone #3** (BL3) - below a skylight provide good light for herbs, fruit, and fruiting vegetables - if the room is hot, avoid growing leafy greens

Partial light zones

These zones include rooms with smallish east or west-facing windows. Crops such as lettuces and others that tolerate some shade do well in these zones. Some sun-loving plants may produce fruit if placed very close to the windows but are not as happy as they would be in a bright light zone. As mentioned above, using grow lights helps in partially lit zones.

- **Partial light zone #1** (PL1) - by or on walls in an east or west-facing room - grow leafy crops, shade-tolerant herbs, lettuce, small root crops, and strawberries

- **Partial light zone #2** (PL2) - in the center of a west-facing room - grow leafy crops, edible flowers like orchids, shade-tolerant herbs, and certain fruit like strawberries.

Note: I have made recommendations in this book for the best growing zones for plants in particular projects. However, it is important to assess your space and know the best places to grow plants within this space. Sometimes you have to move plants in the early stages to find their happy spot!

Things to Know Before you Grow

Once you have established an indoor growing zone map of your home, it is time to get ready to grow. I always remind people to purchase healthy plants and high-quality seeds (if you are starting plants from seeds) for the best results.

Here are a couple of other essential things to know before you grow!

Containers

One of the most important things you can do to ensure your indoor edible garden's success is to choose appropriate containers for your plants. Selecting the right size pot - one that will accommodate the plant's mature size - is vital. Plants with constrained roots don't absorb nutrients or water as they should, which hinders their growth. Large plants and dwarf trees require quite a bit of root room because they live and grow for many years. It is generally necessary to repot these plants as they grow to accommodate their spread.

- **Small containers** - Small containers work well for small herbs and flowers as well as microgreens.

- **Medium containers** - Most indoor edible plants are happiest in a medium-sized container that is at least 10-15 inches in diameter and depth.

- **Large containers** - Large containers that are both wide and tall are great for dwarf trees such as fig or lemon and hold more potting soil. These allow you to water less often.

If you plant moisture-loving plants, avoid clay pots as they tend to draw moisture and dry herbs out quickly.

Drainage

Along with choosing the right sized container, you need to consider drainage carefully. Without proper drainage, roots quickly become soggy, creating an unhealthy environment for plants, and promoting fungal disease and poor growth. Place containers with drainage holes on a pretty saucer or in a pot sleeve where excess water can be collected, or hide plastic planting pots inside a pretty decorative container. If remembering to water is not something you are great at, try a self-watering pot. These handy pots use a wicking system to keep your container plants well-watered.

Finding the Best Pot For your Home Decor

- **_Wood boxes and baskets_** pair great with traditional and farmhouse decor.
- **_Terracotta or glazed ceramic pots_** give off an earthy feel, perfect for a southwestern or rustic home. However, because these pots are porous, don't set them down on delicate surfaces as they may stain.
- **_Metal and faux metal containers_** add interest to contemporary or rustic industrial vibes.
- **_Fiberglass, resin, and plastic pots_** come in all sorts of colors, shapes, and sizes and fit in well with traditional and contemporary homes.
- **_Repurposed containers_** such as old teapots, strainers, and other vintage pots blend in well with rustic home decor. These containers are funky and help to reduce landfill debris.

Planting mixes

Equally as important as choosing the best container is selecting a suitable planting medium. Because your indoor garden plants deserve the best, it is wise not to skimp on your potting mix. It is essential to know your mixes to choose the best one for your edible crops.

- **Seed starting mix** - Seed starting mix is finer than other mixes and allows tiny seeds to contact the soil to help with germination. This is what you need to start any crops from seed. Because this mixture does not usually contain added nutrients, it is not suitable for mature plants. Most seed starting mixes contain a combination of peat or coconut coir, loam, and sand. This type of mix works best for sowing seeds, re-planting young seedlings, or potting cuttings.

- **Multipurpose mixes** - These bagged potting mixes are lightweight and often contain natural materials such as coir, bark, and composted wood fiber. Some also contain added nutrients that help feed plants for a few weeks after planting. This type of mix works well for plants that will be potted for less than a year.

- **Amended mix** - Amended mixes mimic natural garden soil rich in organic nutrients. Along with time-release plant food, amended potting mixes also contain grit and sand, making them quite heavy. This type of mix works well for perennial crops that stay in the pot for more than one year, as well as fruit trees.

- **Acidic mix** - Acidic potting mix is similar to multipurpose mixes, but it has an extra acidic kick, making it perfect for acid-loving plants like oranges, lemons, kumquats, and limes. There is generally enough food to feed plants for a short time. This additional fertilizer is needed to keep acid-loving plants happy and producing.

Additives

Several additives can be mixed into your choice of potting mix to help with growth and add aesthetic value.

- **Perlite & vermiculite -** Perlite is a naturally occurring mineral that is a type of volcanic glass heated to form a whitish grain. Vermiculite is another very lightweight mineral. When added to potting mixes, vermiculite and perlite help improve soil structure and enhance water and soil absorption.

- **Horticultural gravel -** Adding some of this fine gravel to the bottom of planting pots creates a way for water to drain. It also helps support plant roots and potting media while preventing "soggy feet."

- **Sand -** When planting drought-tolerant plants such as Mediterranean herbs, add some sand to your potting mix to create ideal growing conditions.

- **Mulch -** Adding some mulch, such as wood chips, gravel, crushed seashells, glass, or recycled materials, to potted plants adds a decorative touch and helps the soil retain moisture.

Grow Lights

It is possible that you may not have enough natural light to grow certain plants all year long - especially if you live in the north and have a long winter. Thankfully, there are many great choices for supplemental lighting that make it super easy to grow food indoors, no matter where you live.

Choosing the best light can be a bit challenging but don't be dismayed. There are lots of options, depending on the size of your system and what you are growing. When growing edible crops indoors, the main objective is to imitate outdoor light. Provide 14-18 hours of bright artificial light. Keep in mind that the darkness is just as vital as the light. Just like animals, plants need time to rest and metabolize.

- **54 Watt High Output Fluorescent T5** - Fluorescent lights are acceptable for lettuces, leafy greens, and most herbs. They work well for starting seedlings and cuttings and are the least expensive light you can buy for hydroponic growing. These lights' downside is that they don't have the right spectrum for fruiting vegetables and flowering plants. If you are just going to grow leafy veggies, lettuces, spinach, chard, herbs, etc., fluorescent light works fine and will help combat a dark environment. For best results, keep the lights 4 inches to 6 inches above plants. Don't worry; these are cool lights that won't burn the plants. Use 40 watts per square foot of gardening space.

- **H.I.D. (High-Intensity Discharge)** - These lights put out quite a bit of heat, but they are the best lamps available for indoor hydroponics gardens. You can grow any leafing, flowering, or fruiting crops under these lights because they simulate the right spectrum needed and almost mimic what the sun provides. There are two types of bulbs available, MH (metal halide) and HPS (high-pressure sodium). The MH is an excellent all-around light and is fine for most veggies. If your budget only allows for one bulb, get a metal halide one. You can generally find a good 400 watt MH lamp with a bulb for about $140. The HPS bulb is best for the flowering/fruiting stage of vegetables but is not entirely necessary. If you can afford to purchase a conversion lamp that takes both bulbs, that is great. Use the MH for the vegetative growth stage and switch to the HPS when the flowers appear. You can generally find a good conversion lamp including both bulbs for about $200.

- **LED Grow Lights -** LED stands for light-emitting diode. The nice thing about these bulbs is that they use about half of the electricity of traditional lighting. Plus, the bulbs last for a very long time, and they provide cool lighting that won't burn your plants. It is important not to purchase super cheap LED lights that make big promises. In this instance, you do get what you pay for. A good mid-range system will cost between $350 and $500. Keep in mind, LED's will cost most upfront but offer energy savings in the long run.

Airflow

When edible plants are grown out of doors, there are generally no issues with airflow. However, growing indoors, especially with the windows closed, is a different story. Unlike houseplants, edible plants need airflow to grow correctly. Proper air circulation inside the home needs to mimic outdoor air conditions. Without ventilation, the risk of bacterial problems and pest problems is higher. If you have a cross breeze during nice weather, that will do the trick. If the windows need to be closed, utilize small fans to keep air flowing.

Humidity

Like airflow, humidity control is also a big part of indoor growth. In some cases, like when starting seeds, lots of humidity is great, but it can spell disaster in other situations. My favorite place to start seeds is in the bathroom. For maturing plants, locate a spot where there is lots of natural humidity or where you can create humidity with a humidifier.

Pollination

You might be wondering...do I have to pollinate any of my indoor edible plants? This is an excellent question, indeed. When it comes to pollination, you will find two types of plants:

- **Self-pollinating plants** - These types of plants do not need wind, bees, or other insects to produce fruit.

- **Cross-pollinating plants** - These types of plants do need assistance carrying the pollen from the male part of the plant (anther) to the female part of the plant (stigma).

Let's take a closer look at both of these types of plants.

Self-pollinating plants

Most plants, including tomatoes, peppers, beans, and peas, are self-pollinating. However, doing a few small things will help with pollination and encourage fruiting. This includes turning on a fan (like an oscillating fan) in front of the self-pollinating plants, helping flowers with both male and female parts pollinate more frequently. The fan simply gives flowers a little shake, which allows the pollen from the anther to reach the stigma more easily. Even slightly shaking self-pollinating plants by hand can accomplish the same thing.

Cross-pollinating plants

These plants have male and female flowers. Examples of these types of plants include cucumber, melon, and eggplants. Pollen must travel from the male flower to the female flower to produce veggies and fruit. This is the job that bees and other pollinators accomplish so well in the great outdoors. With no bees inside your home (hopefully), the task is up to you. The best method I have found is to use a small paintbrush to lightly collect the pollen from the male flower and brush it onto the female flower's stigma.

How do I tell the difference between a male flower and a female flower?

This is an excellent question and an important one for pollinating reasons! Find the flower with the stamen, and you have located the male; find the flower with the pistil, and you have located the female. Hint: Female flowers have ovaries behind the blossoms that look like baby cucumbers.

Male & Female Flowers

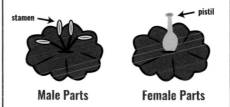

stamen →   ← pistil

Male Parts   Female Parts

Let's get growing

On the following pages you will find the best plants for growing indoors and the zones where you will have the most success. You will also find some easy and creative projects that allow you to grow your favorite herbs and edible flowers all year long indoors.

HERBS AND EDIBLE FLOWERS

Growing herbs is a rewarding experience that can also be quite practical. Herbs have a long history of both culinary and medicinal use. Loading your indoor garden up with a few powerhouse herbs and edible flowers offers incredible beauty and a treasure trove of therapeutic benefits.

Here are a few other things I have learned growing herbs and edible flowers over the years that will help your herb-growing experience be fun and rewarding.

- Pick herbs and edible flowers often. Although you may be tempted to let plants get big and tall, picking them will result in a fuller and healthier plant.

- Don't pick stems from the plant's base; this will cause the plant to grow tall and lanky. To harvest herbs correctly, pick off each stem's tip about one or two inches above a pair of leaves. Doing this will promote new shoots from each stem and produce a healthy and bushy plant.

- For edible flowers, simply snip the entire flower from the stem using clean, sharp scissors.

- Plant selection matters. Picking the healthiest from the start will help ensure that your adult plant is also healthy and productive. Purchase your herbs and flowers from a reputable grower or start with high-quality seeds.

Feed herbs and edible flowers using a half-strength liquid seaweed or worm tea every three weeks. Liquid seaweed is loaded with minerals and trace elements that boost herb and flower growth and promote great flavor.

....

"Life begins the day you start a garden."

-Chinese Proverb

....

Growing multiple herbs and edible flowers in the same pot can make a beautiful display. Be sure to pair herbs that have similar light and water requirements together. Also, pair plants based on their mature size, and be sure to give them plenty of room for expansion.

Edible flowers and herbs do well in bright light conditions (BL 1,2,3) but will also tolerate areas with partial sunlight (PL 1, 2). For darker areas in your home, use grow lights.

The Best Potting Mix for Herbs

Regular garden soil is too heavy for container herbs. Instead, choose a lightweight potting medium that will retain moisture and drain well. Here is my favorite mixture that I use for my potted herbs:

- One part commercial potting mix
- One part aged manure
- One part coarse sand

This mixture is light, nutrient-rich, and drains great!

PROJECT #1:
CEDAR WINDOW HERB BOX

Skill level: Easy
Cost: $$
Plants: Herbs
Growing zones: BL 1, 2 & PL 1
Supplemental light: If lacking sunlight, use grow lights

This darling window herb box garden fits in with any decor and works well in a sunny window. Just be sure to keep herbs moist and rotated so that they don't grow lopsided. Choose your favorite herbs and snip them right before cooking for a fresh and delicious addition to any meal.

WHAT YOU NEED

- 1x4-inch boards, 14 inches long x 3, for sides and bottom
- 1x4-inch boards, 5 inches long x 2, for end pieces
- coconut oil

- clean rag
- 1 ½-inch finish nails
- hammer
- planted herbs and metal pots

HOW TO MAKE IT

1   Attach the two side pieces to the bottom piece using nails.

2   Attach the two end pieces to form an open box.

3   Oil the box with coconut oil and wipe off excess.

4   Place herbs in pots and put them inside the box.

5   Place the box in a sunny location (BL 1, 2) and keep the soil moist but not soggy.

Master Tip: Line the box with a piece of heavy plastic and put some small rocks in the bottom. Plant herbs directly into the box.

How to Grow FREE Herbs

Why buy another herb plant when you can make a second plant from a cutting for FREE? Some herbs like rosemary, marjoram, oregano, thyme, and sage are easy to propagate if you take cuttings from an existing plant. Cut a 2-4 inch piece off a new shoot that does not have any flower buds. Use a sharp and clean cutting blade and cut just below a leaf node, where the leaf is joined to the stem. Be careful not to crush the stem. Cut on an angle to increase the rooting area. Remove the lower leaves, leaving an inch or two of bare stem. Doing this encourages roots to form and reduces the chance of rotting.

Place the cuttings in a lightweight potting medium in a potting tray. Some people like to use root hormone. I am not a huge fan and have never found it to make that much of a difference. After you pot the cutting, place a clear, stiff piece of plastic over the top to create a mini greenhouse. Secure the plastic to the pot using an elastic band. Do not let the plastic touch the cuttings - you may have to support it with small stakes.

Place the pot in a place where it gets bright light but not in direct sunlight. Keep the growing medium moist but not soaked. Most cuttings will root within three weeks. Once you see new growth, put the cuttings in individual 4-inch pots in a bright light area, and continue to keep the potting medium moist.

Project #2: Contemporary Cake Pan Planter

Skill level: Easy
Cost: $
Plants: Mint
Growing zones: BL 1, 2, 3
Supplemental light: If lacking sunlight, use grow lights

Want to celebrate the modern feel of your home? What better way than to grow and display beautiful mint in contemporary, easy-to-make cake pan planters? When grouped, these planters make a spectacular display on a kitchen wall or anywhere that receives bright light for at least six hours each day. If you don't have any extra cake pans lying around, visit your local thrift store, where you are sure to find some.

WHAT YOU NEED

- baking tin - 8 inches or bigger
- permanent marker
- white decorative gravel, small
- potting mix
- plants
- polymer plastic sheet
- ruler
- scissors
- Gorilla glue

HOW TO MAKE IT

1 Place the baking tin face down on top of the plastic sheet.

2 Trace the outline of the pan on the plastic sheet using a permanent marker.

3 Carefully cut out the circle. Find the halfway point and draw a straight line using the ruler.

4 Cut the circle in half. You will use one semicircle per baking pan.

5 Lay the plastic semi-circle over your pan and mark where it ends on each side of the pan.

6 Spread a thin layer of Gorilla glue on the edge of the pan where the plastic will sit. Put the plastic piece on the pan. Press hard to get a good seal. It will dry in about 30 seconds.

7 Add about 2 inches of white stones to the bottom of the cake pan. This will help with drainage.

8 Add a layer of lightweight potting mix and plant your herbs.

9 Lean this planter up in the corner of your kitchen counter or attach it to the wall.

Master Tip: There are several types of delicious mints to choose from, including chocolate mint, spearmint, apple mint, peppermint, citrus mint, and pineapple mint.

Project #3: Suspended Herb Garden

Skill level: Moderate
Cost: $$
Power tools: No
Plants: Thyme, rosemary, lavender, chocolate mint, lemon verbena, etc.
Growing zones: BL, 1, 2, 3 & PL 1
Supplemental light: If lacking sunlight, use grow lights

What better way to enjoy a fresh, caffeine-free drink than by growing and using your very own tea herbs? To make fresh herbal tea, steep harvested tea leaves in boiling water for five minutes before drinking. Add lemon and raw honey to taste.

WHAT YOU NEED

- two 16x8x¾- inch cedar or pine boards - pre-cut and sanded
- 12 small screw eye hooks
- pliers
- wire cutters
- chain
- 6 herbs in plastic pots with drainage holes
- potting mix
- lightweight decorative faux metal pots x 3-6
- screw-in hanging hook

HOW TO MAKE IT

1   Lay the boards on a flat surface. Screw one eye hook into each corner of the bottom side of the bottom board. Use pliers to secure the hook tightly.

2   Screw eye hooks into the corners of both the top and bottom of the top board. Use pliers to secure the hook tightly.

3   Cut 8 pieces of chain to 12 inches each using wire cutters.

4   Attach four pieces of chain to each eye hook - corner to corner- on the bottom board. Use pliers to secure the chain.

5   Secure the other end of the four pieces of chain - corner to corner - to the bottom side eye hooks on the top board. Use pliers to secure the chain.

6   Attach each of the final 12-inch pieces of chain to the eye hooks on the top of the upper board.

7   Cut a piece of chain that is 20-inches long - more if you have a high ceiling.

8   Gather the chains from the four corners of the top board together and attach them to the 20-inch chain - this will be the hanger.

9   Hang from the ceiling using a screw-in hook at the desired height.

10   Hang the shelf in front of a sunny window or any space where the herbs will receive bright light for at least six hours a day.

11   Place the potted herbs on the shelves - evenly distributing their weight.

12   Water herbs every three days or when the top of the potting mix feels dry. Be careful not to saturate the soil. Harvest leaves once a week.

Master Tip: If you are unable to plant herbs or edible flowers in a container with drainage, be sure to choose drought-tolerant varieties and layer the bottom of the container with small gravel or rocks to help with drainage.

"I grow plants for many reasons: to please my eye or to please my soul, to challenge the elements or to challenge my patience, for novelty or for nostalgia, but mostly for the joy in seeing them grow."

-David Hobson

Project #4:
Bark Mounted Orchid

Skill level: Moderate
Cost: $$
Power tools: No
Plants: Small dendrobium orchid
Growing zones: BL 2, 3

Orchids are a true culinary delight that everyone should experience. Many people are familiar with vanilla - an edible orchid, but orchid flowers have been considered an edible treat long before becoming pretty toppings for cakes and cocktails. All orchids are edible and have flavors that vary from bitter to sweet, depending on the orchid type. They are also loaded with fiber and vitamin C. Mounting an orchid on a piece of bark helps mimic natural growing conditions and makes harvesting a piece of cake. Dendrobium orchids are a group of edible orchids that taste like a mixture of kale and cucumber, which makes them a perfect choice for this project.

WHAT YOU NEED

- "Berry oda" dendrobium orchid - not flowering
- a short piece of wire bent into a hook at one end
- sharp scissors
- bark
- sphagnum moss
- hemp cord
- sprayer
- gloves

HOW TO MAKE IT

1 Water the orchid a few hours before starting the project - the best way to do this is to soak the orchid pot in a bowl of water for an hour.

2 Put on your gloves and take the orchid out of the pot.

3 Use the bent wire to gently knock away any potting soil from the roots. Take your time with this to be sure no potting soil remains.

4 Use clean and sharp scissors to trim the roots to 4 inches in length. Doing this will encourage the formation of new roots. Clean any dead debris from around the plant at this time.

There are many types of dendrobium orchids, but some people are allergic to them. Try a small piece before eating a whole handful, just to be safe. Whichever type you choose, be sure to read the label regarding care. Many orchids like it cool in the winter and warm in the summer. Orchids like "Berry oda" have been bred specifically to tolerate indoor heating but still require lots of humidity and excellent airflow. All orchids like bright light; however, be sure to keep them out of direct sunlight in the summer months.

5   Wrap the roots in moss and secure with a piece of hemp cord. Be careful not to tie too tightly around the roots as this could cause damage.

6   Cut another piece of hemp cord and tie one end around the bark, securing it firmly and leaving the other end to tie around the orchid.

7   Place the orchid on the bark. Attach the root ball by wrapping the hemp cord around it. Again, be careful not to wrap too tightly around the roots.

8   Make two small holes near the top of the bark on either side and tie some hemp through to make a hanging loop. Hang on the wall in a bright room by a window. Since orchids love humidity, the bathroom is a great spot.

9   Harvest flowers as needed.

So Much More Than a Garnish

People who live in Hawaii are said to have enjoyed the taste of orchids since the early 1960s. They eat them in salads and as candies. Orchid bulbs are used to flavor ice cream in the middle east, and the tubers are used to flavor meat sauces in Africa. Singaporeans use beautiful orchid flowers in a popular stir-fry dish along with meat and vegetables. Try battering them and frying them in coconut oil like tempura… yummy!

Master Tip: Mist your orchid once a day from spring through fall and every few days throughout the winter with distilled water. In the spring and summer, drop the entire display into a bucket of water twice a week for 15 minutes. Once in bloom, dilute orchid fertilizer in the bucket and feed once a week. It is best to move your orchid to a cool room with a temperature of no more than 55 degrees in the winter.

PROJECT #5:
NO COST LEMONGRASS

Skill level: Moderate
Cost: $
Power tools: No
Plants: Fresh lemongrass stalks
Growing zones: BL 1, 2, 3
Supplemental light: If lacking sunlight, use grow lights

Lemongrass is a shrubby herb native to tropical areas in Asia and the Indian subcontinent. Dried or fresh lemongrass is frequently used to make herbal tea. In some places in India, lemongrass is considered an essential plant in the mind-body medicinal practice known as Ayurveda. Lemongrass is also a popular culinary herb found in Asian and Thai cuisine.

If you love cooking with lemongrass, you will be happy to know that it is simple to propagate at home. Here's how to do it.

WHAT YOU NEED

- lemongrass stems
- cutting board
- sharp knife
- glass for water

- small planting pots
- potting mix
- large container for mature plants

HOW TO DO IT

1   Place the lemongrass stalks on a cutting board and peel off the outer layer from each of the lemongrass stems. With a sharp knife, cut off the top half of the stems.

2   Place the stems in a glass of clean water and set the glass out in a bright area - away from direct sunlight - for a few weeks. You will see tiny white hairs emerging from the base of the stem - these are roots.

3   Fill some small plastic planting pots with potting mix.

4   Create a hole in the center of the mix and plant the stem. Be careful not to damage the delicate root hairs.

5   Firm up the potting mix around the stem and water it.

6   Keep the plant moist but not soggy, and you will soon see leaves form. When you see roots through the drainage hole at the bottom of the pots, it is time to move your plants to a larger pot. Be sure that this pot also has drainage holes.

7   Place lemongrass plants in a bright and sunny location. Keep the potting soil moist but be careful not to overwater. Feed the plants twice a week and harvest when they are 18-24 inches in height. Cut the entire stem and trim off the leafy top.

Master Tip: This growing method also works with celery, leeks, and green onions.

PROJECT #6:
HERBAL COLD COMPRESS

Skill level: Easy
Cost: $
Plants: Fresh and dried herbs
Use: Reduce inflammation and pain

With many anti-inflammatories on the market, patients have access to dozens of treatment options; however, prolonged use of these drugs leads to a long list of adverse effects. Instead, herbal tinctures are highly effective for internal use, and a cold, herbal compress can be applied externally, reducing symptoms of arthritis, inflammatory eye conditions, and more.

WHAT YOU NEED

- clean cloth
- 2 tablespoons fresh dill
- 2 tablespoons dried lavender
- 2 tablespoons fresh rosemary

HOW TO MAKE IT

1   Pour hot water directly onto your dill, lavender, and rosemary to brew a strong herbal tea. You can also create a little herbal pouch using a muslin bag or gauze.

2   Once you've made a potent blend, cool to nearly freezing temperatures.

3   Soak a clean cloth and apply the herbal compress to the affected area(s).

Master Tip: Leave the compress on for 20 minutes and apply up to three times daily.

"An optimistic gardener is one who believes that whatever goes down must come up."

-Leslie Hall

PROJECT #7: BOHO EDIBLE FLOWER POTS

Skill level: Easy
Cost: $$
Power tools: None
Plants: Edible flower plants like carnation, primrose, mums, or pansies
Growing zones: BL 1,2 ,3, 7 & PL 2

These lacy pots are not only practical but also beautiful. They have a bohemian feel to them and are stunning when placed in a group. Display your favorite edible flowers in these easy-to-make pots. Place them in a room where there is plenty of bright light.

WHAT YOU NEED

- lace in different patterns
- sewing glue
- foam brush
- scissors

- terracotta pots with saucers - small, medium, and large
- lightweight potting mix
- plants

HOW TO MAKE IT

1 Water your chosen plants well.

2 Decide where you want to place lace on your pots - you can cover the whole pot, just the top and the bottom, or use vertical strips of lace to create a unique feel - the sky's the limit.

3 Cut lace pieces for each pot.

4 Brush glue on the first pot and place the lace. Cover the top of the lace with another layer of glue. Let it dry and repeat for the other two pots.

5 Fill the pots with potting mix and plant your edible flowers.

Tips for Growing Edible Flowers

You might be surprised to know that a number of beautiful flowers are edible and have a wide range of very subtle and lovely flavors. Here are some tips for keeping your indoor edible flowers looking and tasting great.

- The majority of edible flowers require a sunny and warm environment to thrive.

- Keep all indoor edible plants well-watered but be careful not to over-water.

- Feed edible flower plants weekly with a balanced fertilizer - unless your potting mix contains time-released feed.

- When harvesting, wait until the blooms are fully opened and harvest flowers and stalks. Doing this will encourage new blooms.

Ginger

Ginger is a flowering tropical herbaceous perennial herb that can be grown indoors all year long in cooler climates. The rhizome - the underground portion of the stem- is the part used as a spice and is sometimes referred to as ginger root. Ginger is delicious fresh, dried, powdered, or as a juice or oil. This fragrant veggie is high in a substance called gingerol, which has potent anti-inflammatory and antioxidant properties.

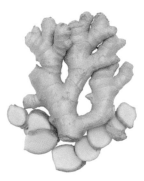

PROJECT #8: HYDROPONIC SPROUTED GINGER

Skill level: Easy
Cost: $
Power tools: No
Plants: Ginger root
Growing zones: BL 1, 2
Supplemental light: If lacking sunlight, use grow lights

If you love ginger - and you should - it's time you learned just how easy it is to grow it at home with a piece of ginger from the grocery store. As long as the pieces are firm, plump, and healthy, they will work. The nubs or buds on the ginger root are like those on potatoes - they will grow roots when conditions are just right

WHAT YOU NEED

- piece of organic ginger - about the size of your thumb with several buds and very healthy

- bowl

- water

- lightweight potting mix

- shallow, wide growing bowls - ginger roots spread horizontally

- organic compost

- organic plant food

"A garden is a grand teacher. It teaches patience and careful watchfulness; it teaches industry and thrift; above all it teaches entire trust."

-Gertrude Jekyll

HOW TO DO IT

1   Place the ginger piece in a bowl and cover it with water. Set the bowl in a plastic bag to create a humid environment. Change the water daily.

2   New ginger stems will begin to form from the nodules.

3   Carefully snap off the new stems and root masses once the stems are about 4-inches tall.

4   Put the old ginger back into the water for more stems to form.

5   Separate each ginger stem if the roots are tangles. Make sure each stem has a good amount of roots.

6   Fill planting bowls with a rich potting mix.

7   Place the ginger root with the eye bud and sprouted stem pointing up and cover it with 1-2 inches more soil. Water lightly.

8   Put the bowl in a spot where it stays warm and doesn't get a lot of bright light.

9   Keep the soil moist, being careful not to over-water.

10   You must be patient; ginger takes time to grow.

11   After about 3-4 weeks, you can harvest small pieces of ginger.

12   To harvest, move the soil at the edge of the pot and slightly lift the ginger piece that has grown. Use a clean and sharp knife to cut off the desired amount of stem towards the pot's edge and replace the potting mix to allow it to grow again.

13   Keep doing this for an endless supply of ginger all year long.

Master Tip: Ginger is a heavy feeder and needs a lot of room to grow, so don't crowd.

SPROUTS

If you are an impatient gardener, sprouts are for you. Most sprouts are ready to eat in as little as three days! Sprouts are simply the very beginning growths from a seed. When the dormant seed begins to "hatch," so to speak, it activates many metabolic systems that eventually help form the first green buds. If this seed were planted, the sprout would be the very first hint of plant life emerging through the soil. When you sprout seeds, you don't plant them. Instead, you encourage these metabolic pathways to begin activation by keeping them moist in a soil-free environment. Once the seed sprouts its first buds, it is ready to eat.

The buds, or sprouts, contain high absorbable protein levels and increased amounts of nutrients like calcium, potassium, iron, and vitamins A, B1, B2, B3, and C, and some of the highest levels of antioxidants around. As the plant continues to grow, these concentrations begin to dwindle. In essence, the sprouts contain the highest concentrations of all the plant's nutrients needed for full growth, which means that they are often even more nutritious than the mature plants.

Sprouting is also inexpensive, and unsprouted seeds can be purchased and stored for an extended time. Another benefit is that sprouted grains contain less starch and gluten than their mature counterparts, making them useful in controlling blood sugar and a better option for those with gluten sensitivity.

> **"Coffee. Garden. Coffee. Does a good morning need anything else?"**
>
> *-Betsy Cañas Garmon*

Project #9:
Speedy Jar Sprouts

Skill level: Easy
Cost: $
Power tools: No
Plants: Seeds for sprouting
Growing zones: BL 2, 3 & PL 1, 2

WHAT YOU NEED

- clean mason jar
- screen mason jar lid
- seeds
- bowl
- non-chlorinated water

HOW TO DO IT

1   Rinse and soak your seeds overnight at room temperature in a bowl of clean, non-chlorinated water.

2   The next morning, dump the water, rinse and place the seeds in a clean Mason jar with a screened lid. The seeds should remain moist but not covered in water.

3   Repeat this process once or twice daily to keep the seeds from molding as they begin to sprout. Pour the water through the screen to rinse the seeds. Allow the jar to sit upside down at an angle so the water can continuously drain. Within a few days, you will begin to see the early blooms.

4   As the sprouts grow and turn green, they are ready to eat. This usually occurs within three to five days. Once you are satisfied with their growth, dry them thoroughly, and store them in the refrigerator.

5   Sprouts will usually keep refrigerated for a few days, but you will want to consume them early to avoid bacterial growth. Add them to salads, soups, sandwiches, and anything you can think of for an incredible nutritional punch you won't find in the produce aisle.

Master Tip: To avoid contamination issues, be sure to clean your sprouting jar exceptionally well before using it. You can soak it in a bowl with hot water and a splash of bleach for 2 minutes to be sure that it is bacteria-free.

Best Sprouts to Sprout

There is a wide variety of sprouts to choose from, each with a unique flavor and texture.

- **Mung bean** - Mung bean sprouts have a unique flavor and crunchy texture, which lands them the title of most popular sprout in the world.

- **Broccoli** - Broccoli sprouts prefer cool conditions. Be sure to provide an extra rinse if you are sprouting in the warmer summer months.

- **Green lentils** - Choose from a variety of lentil colors. These sprouts have a mildly nutty flavor and pair well with soups and salads.

- **Alfalfa** - Alfalfa seeds are amongst the quickest to sprout and taste great on sandwiches.

- **Chickpeas** - Sprouted chickpeas are loaded with protein and add bulk and nutrients to any dish.

MUSHROOMS

Delicious and nutritious mushrooms are a great addition to winter soups, salads, stews, roasts, and stir-fries. No matter what kind of mushrooms you love - oyster, portobello, morel, shiitake, crimini, or classic button - when you throw these gems into any dish, you get great flavor and texture plus a number of health benefits.

The nutritional value of mushrooms is immense. These little fungi contain a range of B-vitamins, including vitamin B12, which is rarely found in vegan sources. They are also rich in minerals, including copper, manganese, phosphorus, potassium, selenium, and zinc. Mushrooms contain an array of phytonutrients, which have been linked to supporting optimal immune function, among many other benefits.

Good news for mushroom lovers: you don't have to settle for store-bought. They are really easy to grow at home!

What's the problem with simply going out and buying mushrooms? Well, for starters, it is essential to buy organic mushrooms. They are incredibly absorbent, and they readily take in whatever nutrients (and toxins) they are grown in. Organic mushrooms are grown without pesticides and chemical fertilizers, but they can be quite expensive, especially for certain varieties such as shiitake.

When you grow mushrooms at home, you can control the growth medium, and rest assured knowing that no pesticides or other chemicals will end up on your plate. You'll also gain the satisfaction of eating something that you have grown yourself with love and care.

Spores in the wind

Like the fruits that the tree produces, mushrooms are the reproductive fruits of 'mycelium' - a dense root-like network of cells. In the great outdoors, the network grows in all directions as it breaks down food into smaller molecules to fuel its growth. Once it runs out of food or is under stress, it goes into survival mode and produces mushrooms so that spores will be taken in the wind to a new home. Pretty cool, right?

Choosing the Best Mushrooms to Grow

When selecting which type of mushroom you want to grow, it is important to choose the right mushroom starter for your chosen growing medium. Some do well in straw, while others prefer to grow in sawdust.

- **Sawdust** - Sawdust is economical and accessible. Most garden stores sell bags of sawdust. It is crucial to get the finest grade sawdust that you can find. Shitake and wine cap mushrooms both do well in sawdust.

- **Straw** - Straw holds moisture well and allows for adequate airflow, making it an excellent medium for growing mushrooms. Wheat straw is the best choice for mushroom cultivation. Oyster mushrooms grow very well in straw.

- **Hardwood block** - If you are new to mushroom growing, a "tabletop" mushroom farm is a great idea. This is a piece of an inoculated log or a hardwood sawdust block. All you do is add water and follow the enclosed instructions to grow delicious mushrooms.

Project #10:
Oyster Mushrooms in Coffee Grounds

Skill level: Easy
Cost: $$
Power tools: No
Plants: High-quality oyster mushroom spawn
Growing zones: BL 2 & PL 1, 2

Maybe you never thought of becoming a mushroom farmer, but I have to tell you, it is so much fun. This project takes advantage of something that you probably throw away daily - coffee grounds. What better way to upcycle spent grounds than to use them as mushroom growing media? Growing mushrooms in used coffee allows you to skip several steps that are necessary when using other growing media. For instance, straw has to be pasteurized before inoculation. Coffee grounds are already pasteurized and loaded with nutrients that oyster mushrooms love.

WHAT YOU NEED

- 2.2 pounds of spent coffee grounds

- 3.5 ounces oyster mushroom spawn

- spawn bag with a filter patch - increases chance of success by reducing contamination

- Large, clean mixing bowl

HOW TO MAKE IT

1. **Collect coffee** - The best place to get coffee is at your local coffee shop. Most will be happy to give you what you need. It must be fresh right before you start the project.

2. **Mixing** - Wash your hands and lower arms and dry. Place the spawn in the bowl and break it up. Next, add the coffee and combine the spawn and coffee well.

3. **Bag it** - Pour the mixture of spent coffee grounds and spawn into the bag and seal it tightly.

4. **Placement** - Place the bag in a warm (64 -75 degrees F) and dark place like under a bed, in a heated dark room, or in a cupboard in a heated room.

5. **Colonizing** - In a few weeks, the coffee grounds will turn white as the spawn colonizes. Once it has fully colonized, everything will be white.

6   **Fresh air -** Place the bag where it will get plenty of fresh air and a little light - a shaded windowsill or table is ideal.

7   **Humidity -** Cut a 2-inch x 2-inch hole in your bag and spray water into the hole twice a day - mushrooms need damp and humid conditions to grow well.

8   **Harvesting -** After seven days, you will see small mushrooms growing. They will double in size every day. Once the edge of the caps turns upwards, they are ready to harvest. Cut at the base of the stems and enjoy!

Master Tip: If you see a green spot mixed in with the white, it is a competitor mold. If the patch is small, add a little salt to the area, killing it off and allowing the mushrooms to grow. If your entire bag is green, you will need to throw it away - poor quality spawn or mold spores in the coffee grounds cause this to occur. With excellent quality spawn, good hygiene, and fresh coffee grounds, this should not happen.

GREENS

If you only grow one thing in your home garden, it should be greens. There are several delicious and nutritious leafy greens that are easy to grow. Leafy greens are also known as salad greens, pot herbs, vegetable greens, or just greens. These plant leaves are eaten as vegetables and contain essential vitamins and nutrients. You probably don't eat enough greens, and unfortunately, the ones you do eat are likely not nearly as healthy as they could be.

Growing greens at home is one of the best things you can do for your health and the health of your family. If you are plugged into the news at all, you will be familiar with the fact that there seems to be an ever-increasing number of food recalls involving greens such as lettuce and spinach. It seems that the greens you find in your local grocery store are prone to contamination from dangerous bacteria. This alone is a very good reason to take greens growing into your own hands.

The good news is, it is super easy to produce crops of greens all year long. The trick to successfully growing greens 365 days per year is knowing which greens to grow and how you can cultivate them indoors. My favorite indoor greens include lettuce, kale, spinach, and microgreens.

Microgreens

No indoor edible garden would be complete without a tray or two of microgreens. Microgreens are among the easiest indoor crops to grow and are chock-full of health benefits since they are the nutrient-dense seedlings of edible vegetables and herbs.

Like sprouts, many microgreens have more nutrients than their adult counterparts! If it wasn't already obvious, I am somewhat of a microgreen fanatic. In fact, I love microgreens so much that I wrote an entire book about them called *Mastering Microgreens*.

Microgreens are super easy to grow and are the perfect solution for the novice or on-the-go gardener. Growing microgreens is super fast and does not require you to invest in any significant equipment or create an entire garden.

If you have a sunny window and a desire to experience the joy of microgreens, you can grow these little gems. The best thing is that you don't have to wait 30 to 60 days to enjoy your freshly grown microgreens; they are generally ready to harvest in as little as **five days after germination.**

With good light and adequate moisture, anyone can grow microgreens from seeds. Although there are some variations when growing different microgreens, such as the best medium to grow in and blackout time, many other elements are similar. Generally, if you are set up to grow one type, you can successfully grow many types.

Are Microgreen Seeds a Thing?

Although many companies will market "microgreen" seeds, there is no such thing. Microgreens are grown from almost any seed and represent the first stage of plant growth. Also called cotyledons, the first leaves of seedlings are followed by a plant's true leaves, and then the plant turns into a vegetable, herb, or fruit. Microgreens are the cotyledon and first true leaves of a plant.

Microgreens are highly versatile and taste great in soups, stews, egg dishes, salads, juices, smoothies, and on top of pizza.

"God Almighty first planted a garden. And indeed, it is the purest of human pleasures."

-Francis Bacon

PROJECT #11:
MICROGREENS 2 WAYS

Skill level: Easy
Cost: $
Power tools: None
Plants: Seeds - radish are super easy to grow
Growing zones: BL 1, 2, 3 & PL 1
Supplemental lighting: If lacking sunlight, use grow lights

Although there are several ways to grow microgreens, it is best to use a shallow tray growing system.

Potting Mix Method

WHAT YOU NEED

- **10x10x1-inch grow tray with drip tray**
- **lightweight potting medium**
- **seeds**

HOW TO DO IT

1   Poke a few small holes in the bottom of your container.

2   Cover the bottom of your container with an inch of moistened potting soil. Flatten it with your hand or a small piece of cardboard to remove any water pockets. Be careful not to over compress.

3   Scatter the seeds evenly on top of the soil. Press them into the soil gently using your hand or a piece of cardboard.

4   Cover your container for blackout purposes.

5   Uncover and mist your seeds a couple of times a day.

6   Remove the cover and expose your microgreens to bright light after they have sprouted.

7   Water as needed to keep moist.

8   Taste your microgreens as they mature and harvest when they're ready by cutting just above the soil line with clean scissors.

The Hydroponic Method

WHAT YOU NEED

- 10x10x1-inch grow tray- no holes
- hydroponic mat
- seeds

HOW TO DO IT

1   Pour one cup of water into your tray bottom.

2   Place your hydroponic mat in the tray and allow it to soak up the water.

3   Spread seed evenly over your mat. Keep in mind; the more seeds you spread on your mat, the denser your crop will be. Be careful not to let your seeds clump.

4   Mist seeds thoroughly, cover, and place in a temperate location (not by a heater or a drafty window).

5   Uncover and ensure that there is always a little water under the growing mat.

6   Once sprouts root, remove the cover and expose it to light.

7   Taste your microgreens as they mature and harvest when they're ready by cutting just above the soil line with clean scissors.

Master Tip: The best way to keep microgreens fresh is to store them in a glass container or jar. After harvesting, put fresh microgreens in a Mason jar or a Pyrex container with a lid. They will keep fresh for up to three weeks in the refrigerator.

Top 3 Microgreen Questions

Are microgreens susceptible to disease? If you follow sowing density rates and have good air ventilation, clean equipment, and do not overwater, your microgreens will stay happy, healthy, and disease-free.

Do I have to fertilize microgreens? Technically, microgreens only need sunlight and water, as they contain all that they need to sprout, grow, and survive. Some people use a diluted fertilizer, but it is not a requirement for success.

Will cooking microgreens destroy the nutrients? Cooking will slightly reduce the nutrient content, but there are ways to cook micros that retain nutrients. A popular method is to stir-fry them lightly in a sautee pan.

Wheatgrass: The Power Micro

Wheatgrass* is a source of living chlorophyll with more health benefits than you can imagine. It boasts many vitamins, including vitamins A, C, and various essential B vitamins for your health. Wheatgrass increases the production of red blood cells, is excellent for thyroid health, detoxifies your liver, and is an excellent natural supplier of oxygen to the blood. Like other microgreens, the nutrients in wheatgrass are so concentrated that many people add them to smoothies or juices. Wheatgrass shots are super popular and provide a quick burst of nutrients and energy. The good news is, growing wheatgrass at home is easy, and these tasty greens are ready for harvest in as little as ten days!

* wheatgrass does not contain any gluten and is safe to consume on a gluten-free diet.

Project #12: Rustic Wheatgrass Centerpiece

Skill level: Moderate
Cost: $$
Power tools: Miter box and saw
Plants: Wheatgrass seeds
Growing zones: BL 1, 2 & PL 1, 2
Supplemental lighting: If lacking in sunlight, use full-spectrum grow lights

Here is an attractive and practical way to grow wheatgrass and bring some green to your table centerpiece!

WHAT YOU NEED

- 1 dog eared cedar fence slat 1" x 4" x 8'
- miter box and saw
- wood glue
- sandpaper
- tape measure
- staple gun and staples
- clear plastic
- hammer and nails
- coconut oil
- potting soil or jute grow mat

HOW TO MAKE IT

1. Measure and cut out three 18-inch pieces from the cedar slat - measure from the straight end of the slat.

2. Set your pieces up so that you have one for the bottom and two for each side.

3. Measure and cut the remainder of the slat to make the end boards flush with each side.

4. Run some glue along the side of the bottom and line up the side and hammer it into place. Repeat on the other side.

5. Run some glue around both ends and hammer the end pieces in place - be sure to stagger the nails.

6. Use a soft rag and liberally apply coconut oil to the inside and outside of the box.

7. Cut the plastic and line the inside of the box, stapling it in place.

8. Put 2 inches of lightweight potting mix in the bottom of the box, or well-soaked jute grow mat for soilless growing.

Master Tip: Your furry pets will also love wheatgrass, which provides them with loads of beneficial nutrients and fiber. Eating the grass mimics their natural foraging instincts.

Growing Wheatgrass in 7 Easy Steps

1. Soak wheat seeds - also called wheat berries - overnight for 12 hours in a bowl of water. The wheat will swell up to double or triple in size.

2. Pour a little water over the potting mix, so it is wet but not soggy. If using a grow mat, soak the mat for twenty minutes and squeeze out extra water. Place the mat in the box.

3. Spread a generous amount of seed over the potting medium or jute mat.

4. Cover the box with a piece of cardboard or a tea towel for three days and then put it in bright light to grow.

5. Mist at least three times a day to keep the potting mix moist.

6. Rotate the box so that it is exposed to the light evenly.

7. Harvest using clean, sharp scissors.

Lettuce

Lettuce is one of the easiest vegetables to grow, providing quick yields without much fuss. To get fresh greens all year, including summer and winter, grow lettuce indoors. Not only is lettuce easy to grow outdoors, but it's also low-maintenance and straightforward inside. Having a fresh supply of delicious lettuce on hand will ensure that you get to enjoy all of the fantastic textures, colors, and tastes that it offers. All types of lettuce are packed with fiber, water, and essential nutrients, including potassium and calcium.

There are records showing lettuce cultivation back to 500 B.C. However, we can thank Columbus for introducing this popular salad and sandwich staple to America in the 15th century. Lettuce is a good source of vitamin C, fiber, iron, and folate. Studies show that lettuce also contains several bioactive compounds with anti-inflammatory, cholesterol-lowering, and anti-diabetic properties.

The four basic groups of lettuce include butterhead, crisphead, celtuce, romaine, and looseleaf. Of these, looseleaf is by far the easiest and most reliable. It is best to choose "little" or "baby" types, which are smaller and easier to grow indoors. Excellent varieties include:

- **Tom Thumb** - Plants produce crisp, buttery leaves and form a loose head.

- **Baby Oakleaf** - Loose, frilly leaves grow from a single stalk.

- **Salad Bowl** - Attractive oakleaf with tasty, succulent, apple-green leaves.

Project #13: Strainer Lettuce Bowl

Skill level: Easy
Cost: $
Power tools: No
Plants: Lettuce seeds
Growing zones: BL 2 & PL 1, 2
Supplemental light: If lacking sunlight, use grow lights.

With successive plantings, you can have a fresh harvest of lettuce all year long. Baby-sized lettuce is ready to harvest in as little as 4-6 weeks.

WHAT YOU NEED

- colander, at least 5 inches deep with drainage holes
- clear plastic
- coconut coir plant liner
- lightweight potting mix
- leaf lettuce seeds
- plastic bowl or wrap

HOW TO DO IT

1 Line the colander with a piece of plastic. Set the plant liner inside of the colander. Fill the colander ¾-full with a lightweight potting mix.

2 Dampen soil. Spread seeds thinly over the potting mix and cover very lightly with a little extra dirt. Spray the potting mix until thoroughly wet. Cover the container with plastic wrap or a plastic bowl to create a greenhouse effect.

3 To grow lettuce successfully, you need a minimum of 12 hours of light; 14-16 is ideal. Because there are fewer daylight hours in the winter, supplemental full-spectrum light is necessary.

4 Keep the potting mix moist - spray each morning and when it is dry.

5 Once the seeds have germinated, remove the plastic bowl or cover.

6 Snip out the weaker seedlings.

7 Feed with an organized fertilizer, half diluted, when the first real leaves appear. Repeat weekly.

8 Harvest the outer leaves first. This will allow the inner leaves to continue growing. Enjoy!

Master Tip: Once lettuce gets bigger, water from the bottom by placing the colander in a tub of water and letting it soak up the water for at least 15 minutes. If the container you used for the dome is large enough, simply fill it with water and use it as a self-watering container for the lettuce by setting the strainer inside.

$Budget Stretcher$
Grow Lettuce from Scraps

If you don't want to wait for seeds to sprout, try growing a fresh bunch of lettuce from scraps! This method works with Romaine lettuce, Boston leaf lettuce, and living lettuce.

- Slice the leaves from the stem, leaving about two inches of the base in place.

- Remove all the leafy pieces without cutting into the stem.

- Place the stem in a glass container with shallow sides. The glass needs to be tall enough to support the growing stem.

- Use toothpicks to stabilize bigger stems. Stick a toothpick on each side of the stem at an angle to create a tripod-like stabilizer.

- Fill the container with water - it should reach halfway up the stem.

- Place the container where it will receive at least 4 hours of bright light per day, but beware of direct sunlight, as it can burn the leaves. You can also use grow lights if you don't have sufficient daylight.

- Change the water in the container daily.

- If you live in a dry climate, mist the leaves with water daily.

- In a couple of days, you should spot some new growth.

- If the stem looks moldy, throw it out and start again.

- Add hydroponic plant food to boost growth.

- Harvest young leaves in 10-12 days as soon as they are big enough to enjoy. Don't let them get too big, or they will taste bitter.

- If you use live lettuce - the kind with the roots attached - you can replant it in a potting medium after it has grown slightly.

"I like gardening — it's a place where I find myself when I need to lose myself."

-Alice Sebold

Kale is a tasty and popular green because it's not quite as intense in flavor or texture as others like collards or mustard greens. You can enjoy kale as a baby green with its tender, delicate flavor or eat it when it is mature. Of course, kale is also highly nutritious:

- Kale has just 33 calories per cup.

- One cup has more than 100 percent of the daily recommended value for vitamins A, C, and K.

- One serving of kale also has many B vitamins, calcium, copper, potassium, and magnesium.

- Kale is also rich in fiber and antioxidants.

Need more reasons to grow kale? Greens are among the most contaminated vegetables in terms of pesticides, and organic greens aren't cheap. It's not hard to grow organic kale for much less money. And, you'll get a lot of use out of this green in the kitchen. It's great raw in salads, sautéed, baked as healthy chips, used in stuffing, casserole, soup, and as a wrap for sandwiches in place of bread.

There is more good news, kale is incredibly easy to grow and a great beginner crop. The best two varieties for indoors are:

- **Scotch Kale** - *Dwarf Blue Curled* - This pretty, frilly-leaved dark kale is one of the best types for making yummy kale chips and for greening up your favorite smoothie. It has a compact size, which makes it perfect for indoor and small space gardening.

- **Tuscan** - *Lacinato* - With narrow leaves and a dimpled surface, this kale is also referred to as "Dinosaur Kale." It makes a beautiful ornamental plant and is a delicious addition to any salad.

10 Tips for Healthy Indoor Kale
Growing Zone: BL 1,2,3

- Decide the number of kale plants you would like to grow.

- Count two seeds for each plant - just in case!

- Soak the seeds in a cup of filtered water for 8 hours.

- Place a lightweight potting medium that includes some perlite in a container that is at least 8 inches deep and 8 inches wide. Moisten the mix.

- Sow seeds ½ inch deep and about 6 inches apart.

- Place your growing container where it will get plenty of sunshine. If using grow lights, leave full-spectrum lights on for 10 hours a day.

- Cover the container with plastic wrap to mimic a greenhouse until the plants have sprouted.

- Water when the soil becomes dry. Be sure to keep the soil moist to help with germination.

- Once plants become established, provide a top dressing of worm castings.

- Harvest mature leaves starting from the bottom of the plant.

Caution: Kale does like cooler temperatures, so if your home is above 70 degrees F, it may struggle to thrive.

PROJECT #14:
KICKED-UP KALE CHIPS

Skill level: Easy
Cost: $
Plants: Kale
Use: Delicious anytime snack

These crispy chips have just the right amount of zip and are the perfect replacement for traditional potato chips.

WHAT YOU NEED

- 10 ounces of kale
- 2 tablespoons olive oil
- 2 teaspoons garlic salt
- 1 teaspoon chipotle powder
- 1 cup nutritional yeast

HOW TO MAKE IT

1   Preheat oven to 400 degrees F.

2   Remove stems.

3   Coat the kale with olive oil and toss to coat all of the pieces evenly.

4   Add the remaining ingredients and toss.

5   Spread evenly on two baking sheets and bake for about 15 minutes or until the chips are crispy.

Master Tip: Let your kale chips cool completely before putting them in an airtight container. They will keep for up to three days.

Spinach

Spinach is a cool-season veggie that is in the same family as beets. It grows quite quickly and yields a lot of delicious leaves to enjoy. This leafy green veggie contains an impressive array of vitamins and minerals, including vitamin A, B-vitamins, C, E, and K, along with calcium, choline, iron, folate, magnesium, manganese, phosphorus, potassium, selenium, and zinc. It also contains an array of flavonoid and carotenoid antioxidants, which help protect the body from the onset of chronic disease.

Not only can these nutrients support the immune system and protect your heart, but they are also vital to bone health. The vitamin K found in spinach has been found to help prevent the buildup of excessive osteoclasts, which are cells that can deteriorate bones. Spinach may also help to encourage the production of osteocalcin an essential protein for the skeletal system.

Additionally, spinach is the perfect superfood to accompany a workout. It is a natural source of nitrates, which contribute to increased muscle strength and endurance, helping you work out longer and harder.

This delicious green can be eaten raw with other veggies, nuts, and a drizzle of coconut oil, added to smoothies, stuffed into organic chicken breasts, or sauteed on its own or with some garlic, to name just a few ideas.

The best thing about spinach is that it does not require a ton of light to grow, and it is well suited for container growing. The main difference between spinach types is taste. Savory types like Bloomsdale have a classic taste, thick leaves, and a generous yield. In contrast, semi-savory types, including Catalina, Teton, and Indian Summer, are easy to grow and are great for beginner gardeners. Smooth-leafed spinach has pretty, flat foliage and includes varieties such as Spac and Red Cardinal - my personal favorite.

Scary Spinach Fact

Supermarket spinach is highly susceptible to salmonella because it has no protective peel. Triple-washed spinach provides even more opportunities for bacteria to flourish since packaging facilities expose it to potentially contaminated equipment before shipping it around the country. A few excellent reasons to grow your own!

Growing Spinach Indoors
the Conventional Way
Growing Zone: BL 2,3 & PL, 1

Spinach is a very forgiving plant and is relatively easy to start from seed. Here are some tips to ensure that your spinach will flourish indoors. Spinach takes between 40 and 45 days from planting to harvest and is well worth the wait.

- Use a high-quality lightweight potting mix that is loamy and has a neutral pH.

- Fill a tray that is at least 6 inches deep with a potting mix. Be sure that the tray has drainage holes.

- Mist the surface of the potting mix and sprinkle the spinach seeds on the mix. If possible, sow the seeds about 2 inches apart in rows and cover with ½-inch potting mix.

- Slide the tray into a clear plastic bag and seal it or cover the tray with plastic wrap or a humidity dome. This helps keep the soil from drying out. Place the tray somewhere warm to sprout.

- Once you see the seedlings emerging, take the plastic or dome off and set the tray in a sunny location—water when the soil's surface feels dry. If using supplemental lighting, place a grow light a few inches above the leaves. Keep in mind that spinach prefers temperatures between 50 and 75 degrees F and needs protection from the hot, direct afternoon sun.

- When seedlings produce their second set of true leaves, remove the excess spinach plants, and ensure that the plants are spaced about 4 inches apart in rows.

- Feed plants with an organic, all-purpose water-soluble fertilizer diluted to a one-fourth recommended rate.

- Harvest the leaves when they reach 4 to 7 inches long, and the plant has at least six leaves. Start with leaves on the plant's outer part and leave the smaller ones on the inside to continue growing. You should be able to harvest the same plant several times until it stops producing or sets seed.

"There are no gardening mistakes, only experiments."

-Janet Kilburn Phillips

PROJECT #15:
HYDROPONIC SPINACH

Skill level: Easy
Cost: $
Power tools: No
Plants: Spinach seeds
Growing zones: BL 2,3 & PL 1
Supplemental light: If lacking sunlight, use grow lights

Named after horticulturist B.A. Kratky from the University of Hawaii, the Kratky method takes the principles of more extensive hydroponics systems and simplifies the entire process. This fun, soilless growing method requires no power and is a perfect addition to your indoor edible garden.

WHAT YOU NEED

- wide mouth mason jar
- 3-inch net pot
- expanded clay pellets
- young spinach transplant
- water
- hydroponic plant food
- aluminum foil
- sharp scissors

"When the world wearies and society fails to satisfy, there is always the garden."

-Minnie Aumonier

HOW TO MAKE IT

1   Clean a wide mouth Mason jar and let it dry.

2   Snip a ½ -inch hole in the bottom of the net pot.

3   Gently remove the spinach transplant from the potting medium.

4   Lightly brush the soil from the roots until they are clean.

5   Cut a piece of aluminum foil and wrap it around your jar.

6   Fill the Mason jar ¾ full with water.

7   Follow the directions on your hydroponic fertilizer and add the required amount into the water.

8   Thread the roots through the hole in the bottom of the net pot.

9   Set the net pot into the mouth of the Mason jar. The roots should be touching the water.

10 Fill in space around the young spinach plant with expanded clay pellets.

11 Set your jar where it will get about 6 hours of light, be careful not to put it in the hot sun; spinach likes cooler temperatures and some shade.

12 Keep an eye on your solution and refill when needed - leaving about an inch between the waterline and the bottom of the net cup. This allows for air circulation.

13 Begin harvesting your spinach when your plant bushes out and has lots of leaves that are 3-4 inches long. You will generally get two harvests from each plant.

Master Tip: If you use grow lights, keep them on for sixteen hours a day and position close to your plants to encourage bushiness over legginess.

FRUITING VEGETABLES

Fruiting vegetables include plants that bear unsweet fruit such as tomatoes, peas, peppers, cucumbers, zucchini, beans, etc. Although fruiting vegetables take a little longer to mature and require a bit more attention than leafy greens, they are well worth the wait and the effort. Pretty flowers make way for delicious and highly nutritious edible fruit that is an excellent part of a healthy diet. Here are my top favorite fruiting vegetables to grow indoors.

Chili Peppers

Chili peppers are members of the nightshade family of vegetables and relatives of bell peppers and tomatoes. There are numerous varieties of chili peppers that are commonly used as a spice. Chili peppers contain capsaicin, which is responsible for the unique taste of peppers and numerous health benefits. Plus, they contain valuable nutrients, including Vitamins C, B6, K1, and A, along with potassium and copper, and have been credited with everything from boosting metabolism to reducing pain.

Chili peppers are as happy in pots as they are in the garden and will willingly produce if you provide a warm room (at least 77 degrees F) and plenty of sunlight. Because they are not subject to the outdoor elements, it is possible to have a pepper-producing plant all year long. Some great varieties to try indoors include.

- **Lemon Drop** - If you love citrus and peppers, you can have the best of both with this pepper that has just the right amount of heat.

- **Cayenne** - Cayenne is related to the jalapeno and bell pepper and is moderately hot.

- **Bird** - Although the peppers on this plant are small, they are plentiful and excellent when dried or pickled to add heat to salsas and soups.

Growing Hot Peppers From Seeds
Growing Zone: BL 1,2,3

1   Fill a seed starting tray with seed starting mix.

2   Water the tray well and allow the water to drain. The soil should remain moist but not soggy.

3   Sprinkle seeds over the top of the mix and cover the container with a grow dome or a piece of plastic wrap.

4   Because peppers like it hot - a heat mat is a great investment. Pepper seeds germinate at temperatures between 70 degrees F and 85 degrees F.

5   Mist the soil daily to keep the growing climate humid.

6   Sprouts will emerge between one week and six weeks. Remove the plastic wrap,

7   Pepper plants need six hours of sunlight per day (BL 1,2). If this is not possible, use grow lights.

Chili Growing Tips

- Snip the weakest plants early with clean, sharp scissors. This makes more room for healthy plants.

- Place a fan on low speed near the sprouts - this helps the stem grow strong.

- Transplant small pepper plants into containers that are 12 inches wide and 12 inches deep.

- Use a mixture of 40 percent sphagnum moss and 60 percent cow manure for best results.

PROJECT #16:
PEPPER DRYING 101

Skill level: Easy
Cost: $
Plants: Peppers
Use: Preservation

If you live in a dry climate where daytime temperatures are above 85 degrees F, drying peppers is a snap. Here's how to do it.

Step 1: Select: Choose thin-walled peppers; they dry outside the best. Use fresh peppers with no blemishes.

Step 2: Thread: With a long needle and thread, string the peppers through the stem - leave space between the peppers for airflow.

Step 3: Hang: Hang peppers up in a space with adequate airflow and plenty of sunshine.

Step 4: Remove: Remove peppers from the string when they are completely dry and brittle - this may take up to 3 weeks.

Master Tip: If you don't live in an area with warm, dry conditions, use your oven. Set the temperature to 150 degrees F and leave the door open to allow for appropriate airflow. Check on peppers every 30 minutes and remove the dry ones. Drying can take between 1-2 hours.

Peas

Not only are green peas delicious, but they contain a large number of nutrients and antioxidants. Research shows that eating peas can help protect you from chronic illnesses like heart disease and cancer. Green peas are also known as garden peas and are relatively easy to grow in an outdoor garden. Thankfully, they are just as easy to grow indoors if given the right conditions and a trellis structure to climb up.

My top three favorite peas to grow indoors include:

- **Little Marvel peas** - This semi-dwarf plant produces sweet and tender peas. It grows to 30 inches and does not require staking. This pea is perfect for freezing.

- **Dwarf Grey Sugar peas** - This heirloom plant produces plump and tender peas with beautiful purple blossoms. When mature, dwarf grey sugar peas reach a height between 24 and 30 inches.

- **Super Sugar Snap peas** - The snap pea is also known as the sugar snap pea and has edible rounded pods and thick pod walls. A trellis is definitely necessary as it can reach up to six feet.

6 Steps to Sowing and Growing Peas Indoors

1   Sow seeds directly in 4-6 inch pots filled with a lightweight potting medium. Keep the soil moist but not soggy.

2   Grow peas near a sunny window that gets at least 8 hours of full sun per day. Alternatively, use grow lights for 8-10 hours per day.

3   Transfer pea shoots to a larger pot when they are about two inches tall and provide a trellis.

4   Keep the pea vines out of the dirt and gently encourage them to climb.

5   Pinch the tops of stems to discourage legginess.

6   Harvest pea shoots at any time for a delicious salad addition. Pods are ready when firm and green with plump peas inside.

Note: Sow peas every two weeks for a continuous supply.

....

"Many things grow in the garden that were never sown there."

-Thomas Fuller

....

PROJECT #17:
PEAS IN A BOX

Skill level: Easy
Cost: $$
Power tools: No
Plants: Pea seeds
Growing zones: BL 1,2
Supplemental light: If lacking sunlight, use grow lights

This project is so much fun and a great way to grow sweet and delicious peas indoors. Any box or container will work, along with a trellis to support the climbing peas, if needed. This pea box makes a great indoor edible conversation piece.

WHAT YOU NEED

- box of your choosing as long as it is at least 8 inches deep
- heavy-duty plastic
- scissors
- staple gun and staples
- expanded clay pellets or small rocks
- lightweight potting mix with organic fertilizer
- 4 young pea plants
- 4 bamboo stakes
- jute or hemp twine

HOW TO MAKE IT

1. Staple the plastic on the inside of the box as a liner.

2. Cover the bottom in a 1-inch layer of pellets or small rocks to help with drainage.

3. Fill the box with a lightweight potting mix and moisten.

4. Plant one pea transplant in each corner - a few inches towards the middle of the box.

5. Position a bamboo stake in each corner and tie together using twine at the top.

6. Starting at the top of the trellis, run the twine around the teepee style trellis until you are about 2-inches from the potting mix.

7. Position the box where it will receive bright light but not in an overly hot area or under grow lights.

8. Keep the soil moist but not soggy.

Master Tip: Use twist ties or garden twine to hold the pea vines to the trellis as they mature. Just be careful not to tie the vines too tightly as it may injure the plant.

Tomatoes

Tomatoes are a staple plant in almost every veggie patch, and for a good reason. Just one tomato supplies 40% of the daily recommended amount of vitamin C. In addition, tomatoes contain vitamin A, which is great for immunity, skin health, and vision; vitamin K, which keeps your bones strong; and potassium necessary for heart function, muscle contraction, healthy blood pressure, and fluid balance. What's more, tomatoes are excellent raw, dried, or turned into your favorite sauce.

Tomatoes love the warmth and sunshine of summer, and the key to delicious indoor tomatoes is replicating these conditions inside your home. Although fruit production may not be as prolific as plants grown outdoors, you can still enjoy a healthy supply of sweet and delicious homegrown tomatoes when you choose the right varieties. Great types to grow inside include:

- **Tiny Tim** - Dwarf-size plants produce small, delicious cherry tomatoes that make them perfect for containers.

- **Red Robin** - Attractive compact plants produce extra sweet cherry tomatoes.

- **Toy Boy** - This heirloom plant produces fruit the size of a grape on a small plant that grows to about 18 inches in height.

7 Tips for the Best Indoor Tomatoes

1 Tomatoes need at least 8 hours of sunlight daily to thrive (BL 1, 2). If you can't provide this, use a grow light.

2 Use unglazed pots that breathe and have good drainage holes.

3 Plant tomato seeds in a starter mix about ¼-inch deep.

4 Keep the soil moist and warm - a heat mat works great.

5 Keep tomato plants out of drafty locations.

6 To increase your chances of success, try hand pollination. Tap stems lightly when flowers bloom to distribute pollen.

7 Rotate your plant to ensure that it gets adequate light on all sides.

Project #18: Fresh Mango Tomato Salsa

Skill level: Easy
Cost: $
Plants: Tomatoes
Use: Dip your favorite chips or eat as a side salad with seafood or chicken

WHAT YOU NEED

- 1 cup finely diced peeled mango (from a ½-pound mango)
- 2 cups cherry tomatoes sliced in half
- 2 tablespoons minced red onion
- 1 teaspoon minced serrano or habanero chile
- 1 tablespoon fresh lime juice
- ½ teaspoon coconut sugar
- ½ teaspoon unseasoned rice vinegar
- 1 tablespoon chopped cilantro
- 2 teaspoons chopped mint
- Salt and freshly ground pepper

HOW TO MAKE IT

1   Combine the mango with tomatoes, onion, and chile.

2   Stir in the coconut sugar, rice vinegar, lime juice, cilantro, and mint.

3   Season with salt and pepper and serve.

Master Tip: Fill pretty glass jars with this delicious salsa and combine with chips in a gift basket that friends and family will love.

ROOT VEGETABLES

Root vegetables are an edible part of a plant that grows underground. These delicious veggies are rich in soluble and insoluble fiber, which helps to lower blood sugar and blood fats and increase healthy gut bacteria while lowering the risk of Type 2 diabetes, heart disease, and bowel cancer.

Given the right soil depth, many root veggies, including carrots, beets, potatoes, radishes, and sweet potatoes, happily thrive in containers in an indoor environment. Radishes and garlic do well in smaller containers; carrots, onions, and beets require slightly more room, and potatoes need even more container space to spread out. All root vegetables require loose and well-draining potting mix as well as organic fertilizer. Regular, deep watering encourages strong root growth.

My favorite root vegetables to grow indoors include carrots, beets, garlic, and radishes. These indoor edible crops will not disappoint as long as you provide the right conditions.

Knowing when to harvest root veggies can be tricky since you can't see them to determine if they are ripe. The best way to judge when it is time to pull up your harvest is to check the back of the seed package for the estimated harvest date.

Garlic

Garlic, a member of the onion family, contains powerful medicinal properties, including over thirty antifungal, bacterial, parasitic, and viral agents. It is immune-boosting and offers anti-infection properties – plus, it adds fabulous flavor to any dish.

Many people grow garlic indoors for the deliciously edible greens; however, if you are patient, you can grow a full-blown bulb from a garden center clove. This process can take up to six months, but it is fun and well worth the wait.

Growing Garlic Indoors in 7 Simple Steps

1   Choose your garlic. Pick up an organic garlic clove from your favorite garden center, not the grocery store.

2   The pot. A simple clay pot with a drainage hole works best. Cover the drainage hole with a coffee filter.

3   Potting mix. Fill the container up to 2 inches below the rim with a lightweight potting mix.

4   Split the clove. Pry the garlic open into cloves. Try to keep the most skin on as possible. Discard any cloves that are soft or look rotten.

5   Plant. Push one clove per pot into the soil, pointy side up, about halfway down.

6   Sunlight. Move your pot to a sunny location (BL 1).

7   Water. Water the garlic when the potting mix feels dry.

8   Feed. Feed twice a month with a half-strength water-soluble fertilizer.

9   Be patient. As mentioned above, garlic takes a while to develop. When the leaf shoots turn brown, stop watering. In a couple of weeks, the shoots will be dry, and the bulb should be ready to harvest.

The Best Way to Preserve Garlic

A big garlic harvest is great for cooking, but what if you can't use it all before it starts to sprout and gets mushy? Store garlic bulbs as you would onions, in a dry, cool spot, like a basement or cellar. It will last a few weeks this way.

To preserve garlic, if you cannot use it within a few weeks of harvest, you can blend it up and freeze it in airtight containers. You can also dry and store garlic cloves. Unfortunately, these methods have limitations, including diminished flavor. Keeping your garlic in oil is not ideal either, as it can promote harmful bacteria growth, especially at room temperature.

The best (and safest) way to preserve your garlic cloves for months is to store them in vinegar. Unlike other vegetables, when pickled, the vinegar does not overpower the garlic flavor. When you're ready to use the cloves, just rinse them with water. You can also use flavored vinegar for cooking. Here's how to do it:

- Peel only the best cloves, those that are not too soft, bruised, or starting to sprout.

- Rinse the cloves and place them in a glass jar.

- Fill the jar with full-strength vinegar until it fully covers the cloves. You can also use a dry wine.

- Add dried spices and seasonings if you want, but this isn't necessary. Good seasonings for garlic include dried peppercorns, chili flakes, cumin seeds, and bay leaves.

- Seal the jars and label with the preparation date.

- Store the garlic in the refrigerator for up to four months. After that, it could grow mold. Never store vinegar-preserved garlic at room temperature.

Always discard any preserved foods if you see mold or yeast growth or if the jar's top is bulging. In vinegar, your garlic cloves should remain safe and tasty for months.

PROJECT #19:
GARLIC GREENS IN A GLASS

Skill level: Easy
Cost: $
Power tools: No
Plants: Garlic bulbs
Growing zones: BL 1, BL 2
Supplemental light: Full-spectrum light if not enough direct sunlight.

If patience is not your strong suit, growing garlic greens may be just the thing for you. Garlic greens are also known as baby garlic or garlic springs and taste like garlic chives but look like green onions. Softneck varieties work best for greens.

WHAT YOU NEED

- garlic bulb
- paper towel
- clear container
- water

HOW TO DO IT

1   Wrap one or more cloves in a damp paper towel and place it in a warm location. In about two days, the cloves should sprout.

2   Place the sprouted clove in a clear container with the sprouted end pointing upward. A drinking glass or jar works well for multiple cloves.

3   Fill the container with room temperature water. The water level should cover just a little less than half of the garlic sprout.

4   Place the container in a sunny windowsill (BL, 1). There must be at least 12 hours of sunlight per day, so you may have to supplement with grow lights if you live in a cooler climate.

5   If the tops of the garlic sprouts begin to wilt, they may have too much hot sunlight. Remove them from the heat for a day or so, and they should rebound nicely.

6   Replace the water every other day.

7   Once the shoots reach between four and seven inches tall, harvest greens using clean, sharp scissors. Be sure to snip only the top two-thirds of the greens as the lower parts are bitter.

Master Tip: Harvest only what you can eat; fresh garlic greens don't store well.

Radish

Growing radishes is a great experience for first-time gardeners, mostly because they grow so quickly and easily. About four weeks after planting, you will be able to enjoy radishes as part of your bountiful indoor harvest.

Not only are radishes a delicious snack or addition to your favorite salad, but they contain antioxidants and minerals, including potassium and calcium. Together, these nutrients can help reduce elevated blood pressure and improve blood flow. Radishes also contain chemicals that help regulate blood sugar and protect against insulin resistance.

Sow radishes every few weeks for a continual supply of these tasty gems. My favorite varieties for indoor growing include:

- **Cherry Belle** - This fast-maturing, easy-to-grow heirloom radish won't let you down with its crisp and mild flavor.

- **Sparkler** - This brightly colored scarlet radish is juicy with a sweet-tart flavor.

- **French Breakfast** - This beautiful French heirloom radish has scarlet-red skin at the tip that transitions to a white base and a mild taste.

Grow Radishes in 5 Easy Steps

1   Prepare a rectangular growing container that is at least 8 inches deep with a lightweight potting mix.

2   Spray the potting mix. Push seeds lightly into the soil about 2 inches apart. Sprinkle potting mix on top of the seeds. Spray the potting mix so that it is wet but not saturated.

3   Create a mini-greenhouse by covering your container with plastic wrap for a few days. Remove the wrap when you see sprouts. Spray the potting mix.

4   Place the container in a spot where your radishes will receive bright but indirect light (BL 2, PL 1) or under full-spectrum grow lights. Radishes prefer cooler temperatures, so grow them in a cooler room, if possible.

5   Water radishes regularly. Harvest in 3-4 weeks and enjoy.

Top 3 Radish Questions

Why are the leaves on my radish plants turning brown? This is most likely due to a light issue. Radishes prefer cooler temperatures and less direct light. If the leaves begin to turn brown or are droopy, move the container to a cooler location away from direct sunlight. If using grow lights, try moving the light further away from the container.

Why do my radishes taste dry and woody? Most of the time, when radishes taste woody or are dry, they have been left growing too long. Many people think that a good radish has to be big. The truth is, smaller radishes that are harvested within a few weeks (depending on the variety) taste the best. Radishes that are about an inch in diameter are perfect for harvesting.

How do I know when it is time to harvest my radishes? Radishes, like carrots, will "shoulder" when they are ready to be picked. This means that they will push up out of the soil with part of their ruby red showing through. When this happens, it is time to harvest.

PROJECT #20:
ROASTED RADISHES

Skill level: Easy
Cost: $
Plants: Radishes
Use: Great snack or side dish

Radishes are fantastic raw but are equally delicious roasted. Roasting brings out the sweetness of this impressive root crop and lessens the snappy kick that you get when eating it raw. Roasted radishes are similar to roasted potatoes, only lower in carbs and calories.

WHAT YOU NEED

- 1 pound radishes, ends trimmed and halved
- 1 tablespoon melted ghee
- ½ teaspoon sea salt
- ¼ teaspoon pepper
- 3 garlic cloves, finely minced
- ¼ teaspoon dried parsley
- ¼ teaspoon dried chives

HOW TO MAKE IT

1 Preheat oven to 425 degrees.

2 Combine radishes, melted ghee, and salt and pepper, and toss until radishes are evenly coated.

3 Spread radishes out in a 9x13-inch baking dish but don't overcrowd.

4 Bake for 25 minutes, tossing every 10 minutes or so.

5 Add the minced garlic and spices and bake for 5 more minutes until the radishes are golden brown and cooked all the way through.

6 Serve with ranch dressing for a delicious dip.

Beets

Beets are incredibly delicious and taste earthy when raw and sweeter when cooked. They are also super nutritious, containing lots of folate and fiber. Betanin, a phytochemical known to boost immunity, is what gives them their rich, red color. Just one serving can help increase energy levels, reduce blood pressure, and alleviate arthritis pain. The ancient Romans were even said to have used beets as an aphrodisiac.

Beets are a fantastic crop to grow inside, and all parts of the plant are edible. Baby beet greens are loaded with nutrition and ready to enjoy about six weeks after planting. Depending on the variety, young beets are ready as early as 30 days after planting. My favorite indoor varieties include:

- **Detroit Dark Red** - This heirloom beet is one of the most popular beets out there. These beets are dark red and about 3 inches in diameter. Perfect for canning.

- **Golden Boy** - This mild, golden beet does not stain like red beets. It has stunning orange-gold flesh and bright green tops.

- **Chioggia** - This type of beet is so much fun to grow, with its concentric rings of red and white. Also known as the candy cane beet, the Chioggia has a delicious, sweet flavor.

How to Grow the Best Beets Ever

1   Pick the right container and soil. Because you're growing beets for their large roots, you need a pot that is at least 18 inches deep. The container also needs drainage holes. Fill it with a rich, loose potting soil.

2   Plant the seeds. Spacing is essential to growing good beetroots. Place each seed about a quarter-inch deep in the soil and one foot from the next one. Spacing varies a little with each variety, so follow the instructions on the seed packet.

3   Wait for germination. Beet seeds need a few weeks at about 50 degrees Fahrenheit to germinate. Keep the containers in a cool spot until they sprout. Make sure the soil remains moist but not soggy.

4   Provide light and water. Once you have seedlings in the container, move them to a sunny window to get several hours per day of direct sunlight. Water when the top quarter-inch of soil is dry. About an inch of water per week is adequate for beets.

5   Harvest and enjoy. Check the seed packet for the time to maturity to give you a good idea of when the beets are ready. Dig out the roots - which should be about the size of a golf ball - with a sharp hand shovel.

Once your beets are ready to harvest, you can keep the greens on for longer storage or remove them if you plan to use the roots immediately. Beetroots are delicious roasted, and the greens can be sauteed or used in stir-fries.

Project #21:
Beet Seed Tape

Skill level: Easy
Cost: $
Plants: Beet seeds
Use: To make planting easier

Seed tape is an excellent way to plant small seeds that are otherwise difficult to handle.

WHAT YOU NEED

- ruler
- marker
- 2 tablespoons of white flour*

- 1 tablespoon water
- single-ply toilet paper
- beet seeds
- toothpicks

* a great gluten-free option is egg yolk

HOW TO MAKE IT

1   Make seed glue by combining the flour and water. The glue should not be too watery.

2   Roll the toilet paper out to the desired length. If you have 2-ply paper, split it into two layers. Fold the paper in half horizontally and unfold it to create a crease.

3   Check the seed package to see how far apart the seeds need to be. Use a ruler and marker to mark the location within the crease on the toilet paper - start about 1 inch from the edge.

4   Dip the tip of the toothpick in the glue, pick up one seed, and place on each dot on the paper.

5   After placing all seeds, place drops of glue around the perimeter of the paper.

6   Fold the paper in half at the crease to seal the paper. Let it sit for about two hours.

Master Tip: Roll the seed paper up and store it in a cool, dry spot until you are ready to plant. This method works for all small seeds and is a fantastic way to prepare seeds for planting in a space-saving manner.

Carrots

Believe it or not, growing carrots indoors in containers is easier than growing them outdoors. Carrots need consistent moisture to thrive, which is often difficult to achieve in an outdoor setting. Furthermore, because you can control the type of soil that you grow in, container gardens produce carrots without deformities.

Carrots are a beautiful root crop with an endless list of varieties in a rainbow of colors and number of shapes and sizes. Container carrots have beautiful and dainty foliage, which makes them one of the most attractive indoor edible crops to grow.

Adding carrots to your diet provides a plethora of nutritional benefits. Here are just a few.

- Carrots contain nutrients, like vitamin A and antioxidants, that can help protect your skin from sun damage, dullness, and signs of aging.

- Carrots are high in fiber, which can help lower blood pressure and reduce heart disease risk.

- Although carrots are sweet, they are pretty low on the glycemic index, which means you can eat them without worrying about a spike in blood sugar.

- The combination of K1, potassium, and vitamin A promotes healthy bones.

- Your immune system will benefit from the addition of carrots, which contain plenty of vitamin C along with A, B6, and K.

- Carrots are great for eye health because of the high amount of vitamin A - with 210% of the daily value.

Like other indoor edible crops, choosing a smaller variety of carrots with a shorter root system produces the best results. Some of my favorite indoor types include:

- **Danvers** - If you love long and slender carrots, this type is for you. This popular variety grows to about 8 inches in length and is happy in pots at least 10 inches deep.

- **Little Finger** - Grow dozens of these little carrots in an 8-inch wide rectangular planter. These sweet-tasting carrots grow up to 4 inches in length, making them perfect for snacking, canning, or pickling.

- **Chantenay Red Cored** - Kids love the taste of this sweet and heavy-producing carrot. The roots of this small variety only grow about 6 inches in length.

7 Steps to Delicious Indoor Carrots
Growing Zone: BL 2 & PL 2

- Start carrot seeds in a pot or container where they will stay to grow through maturity. This works well because carrots don't like to be transplanted.

- Use a potting mix along with a 5-10-10 fertilizer.

- Plant seeds according to the depth instructions on the package and 2 inches apart. Carrots are planted very shallow, usually just 1/8 inch to 1/4 inch deep.

- Moisten potting mix and drop three seeds into each hole. Cover lightly with potting mix.

- Cover the pot with plastic wrap and place it in a warm, sunny location.

Project #22:
Dainty Carrot Top Garden

Skill level: Easy
Cost: $
Power tools: No
Plants: Carrot seeds
Growing zones: BL 2 & PL 2
Supplemental light: If lacking sunlight, use grow lights

You know those carrot tops that you chop off and throw in your compost or feed to your chickens? These very same tops can be planted to produce a dainty and delicious carrot top plant. Contrary to what you might think, carrot tops are not poisonous! They are entirely edible, with a slight carrot taste and an abundance of nutrients like potassium, chlorophyll, calcium, six times the root's vitamin C, and protein. That is quite a lineup.

WHAT YOU NEED

- carrots
- sharp knife
- growing pot with drainage holes
- lightweight potting mix

HOW TO MAKE IT

1 Cut tops off of carrots so that you have 1-inch pieces.

2 Fill pots about ¾ full with the potting medium.

3 Plant the tops so that a little bit of green is sticking out of the potting medium.

4 Keep the soil moist but not soggy, and place the pot in a sunny window. Greens should be ready to harvest in about a month. You can harvest several times from the same top before needing to replant.

5 Use the tops in soup, salads, stir fry, pesto or juices.

Master Tip: Plant heirloom carrot tops and let the greens flower. Collect the seeds for your garden next year. Also, you can sprout carrot tops in water instead of soil. Just keep the water clean and give the tops plenty of light.

FRUIT

Now that your confidence is boosted by growing great indoor edible crops like lettuce, microgreens, radishes, herbs, and more, it is time to tackle growing fruit indoors. Many people shy away from growing fruit indoors, but in reality, once you have the basics down, it is pretty easy and adds great variety to your indoor edible garden.

Because so many people are hesitant to take on growing fruit indoors, I have structured this section a little differently. You will find a complete guide to growing some of the most popular indoor fruit plants along with troubleshooting, harvesting, use, and preserving tips.

Like any other indoor edible crop, I suggest that you pick one or two types of fruit to start with and once you have perfected those, try others. Selecting the best varieties and following my growing tips below, you will soon be on your way to enjoying delicious fruit from your indoor edible garden.

Even if you choose self-pollinating fruit trees, giving them a little help with pollination will produce a more abundant harvest!

Lemons, limes, and oranges

You don't have to live in Florida or Arizona to enjoy fresh citrus from your tree. Container-grown lemon, lime, and orange trees thrive indoors, given the right conditions. Most dwarf citrus trees are self-pollinating, so no need to worry about hand pollination.

Best indoor varieties

Set yourself up for citrus success by starting with the right variety. Some types of orange, lemon, or lime will do much better in containers and indoors than others. The first consideration is size. Standard-sized trees will be difficult to grow inside, so look for dwarf varieties. Lemons and limes generally need less sunlight, so they often make better choices than orange trees.

With those factors under consideration, here are some of the best citrus varieties for indoor growing:

- **Meyer lemon** - This is an orange-like lemon and one of the most commonly grown citrus trees indoors. It can fruit at any time of year. Look for the 'Improved dwarf Meyer lemon.'

- **Ponderosa lemon** - Another lemon that takes well to containers is 'Ponderosa.'

- **Australian finger lime** - Look for a dwarf or semi-dwarf version of this fruit, also known as citrus caviar. The name comes from the spherical, juicy vesicles inside the limes.

- **Kaffir lime** - This is another variety that does well indoors as a dwarf tree. It's used in Thai cooking.

- **Tangerines** - If you have your heart set on growing oranges, try tangerines. They do better indoors than other varieties.

- **Otaheite orange** - Another orangey option is Citrus limonia. This is a dwarf cross between lemon and tangerine.

- **Kumquats and limequats** - Kumquats are unique little citrus fruits that do well when grown indoors. Also, try the key lime-kumquat hybrid.

Light and heat

Considering these trees grow in the sunshine state, it's no surprise that they need a lot of light to thrive. Find the sunniest possible spot in your house for your citrus tree. South or southwest facing windows are best (BL 1,2,3). They will need an absolute minimum of six hours of bright light a day but ideally ten or more. Use grow lights if your natural light is limited.

The citrus tree will grow most during the spring and summer. This is the time when getting adequate light is most important, so when it's warm enough, move your container outside to get full, bright sun. Start it out in a shady spot so it can get acclimated to sunlight.

The best temperature for a citrus tree growing indoors is 65 degrees Fahrenheit during the day. The temperature should drop five to ten degrees at night. Choose an indoor spot for your tree that includes plenty of light but is away from cold drafts, air vents, and doors to the outside.

Watering

Drainage is essential for a citrus tree. Sitting water will kill it. Use a container with drainage holes and a saucer underneath to catch at least a gallon of excess water. Choose a soil mix that is not too heavy. A good blend is one-part potting soil, one-part perlite or vermiculite, and one-part peat. The peat makes the soil a little acidic (which citrus prefers), while the perlite aids drainage.

With good drainage, you also must get the watering schedule right. Water the tree when the first inch or two of soil is dry. Let the water run through the drainage holes. The watering schedule will vary by season, so use the dry soil test rather than a strict watering time routine.

Mist Citrus In Dry Climates

Mist citrus trees with water regularly in the winter or if you live in a dry climate.

Feeding

Citrus trees are heavy feeders. Nitrogen is vital, but balance is key. An excess of nitrogen will cause the tree to put too much effort into growing leaves rather than flowers and fruits. Look for a product designed specifically for citrus. The best times to feed are before flowering and after fruiting.

"Gardeners, I think, dream bigger dreams than emperors."

-Mary Cantwell

Harvesting

If you do everything right, your tree will reward you with fruit. Timing is essential for the harvest, as citrus fruits do not ripen off the tree. Be patient. It can take six to eight months for the fruit to be ready. Taste is the best indicator of ripeness, so when you think the fruit is ready, remove one with shears and give it a taste.

Be aware that most citrus goes through a fruit drop early in the season. The trees will naturally drop some immature fruits. This does not mean the fruit is ripe or ready to harvest. It is a natural way of thinning weaker fruit so the stronger ones will grow well.

Troubleshooting

Despite your best efforts, problems may arise with your citrus tree:

- **Yellowing, curled leaves, dropped leaves.** This is a common sign of overwatering in citrus. Let the soil dry longer between watering. Yellowing along the veins may indicate inadequate nitrogen.

- **Crisp, dry, drooping leaves.** These are signs of underwatering. Other symptoms include water running straight through the drainage holes and dry soil pulling away from the pot's top edges.

- **Burned edges on leaves.** Over-fertilizing can cause this phenomenon. Another sign is excessively slow growth.

- **Dropped green leaves.** If healthy-looking leaves start dropping, your tree may not be getting enough light.

You may also see pests on your citrus tree like aphids, spider mites, and fruit flies. Rot or fungus indicates disease. Prevent these by providing the right conditions. Check leaves often for pests and wipe them down regularly, both on the top and the undersides.

Creative ways to enjoy your citrus

There are many ways to use citrus fruits, including the obvious. Eat them fresh, use them in juices and cocktails, include the zest in baked goods, and try the fruit and juice in savory dishes and salad dressings. There are many other things you can do with citrus:

- Boil slices in water for an air freshener.

- Microwave citrus slices and then wipe down the inside of your microwave to clean it. It will smell amazing!

- Polish copper pots with lemons.

- Send citrus, baking soda, salt, and water down the garbage disposal to clean it.

- A half a lemon in the dishwasher adds sparkle and a fresh smell.

- An orange studded with cloves keeps moths at bay.

Preserving

You may just get more of a harvest than you can use from your indoor citrus trees. Citrus fruits store well and remain fresh in cool temperatures for several weeks. You can also enjoy the fruit by preserving it:

- Zest the fruit and let it dry before storing it in an airtight container.

- Dry entire peels for later. Or, try candying them with sugar.

- Juice the fruits and freeze for storage.

- Use a food dehydrator to dry slices you can store in jars.

- Make marmalade or curd.

- If you can't use the peels, compost them or use them as seed starters.

PROJECT #23:
ZESTY LEMON SCRUB

Skill level: Easy
Cost: $
Plants: Lemon
Use: For softer hands and feet

This scrub is like a mini spa treatment at home. Use it on your hands and feet for an energizing boost.

WHAT YOU NEED

- **1 cup Epsom salts**
- **2 tablespoons coconut oil**
- **grated lemon peel**
- **juice of 1 lemon**
- **glass container with a lid**

HOW TO MAKE IT

1 Squeeze lemon juice into a bowl.

2 Add the Epsom salts and coconut oil and mix well.

3 Add the grated lemon peel and stir.

4 Place in the glass jar.

Master Tip: Add a few drops of lemon essential oil to your mix for a sweet fragrance that lasts a long time.

Strawberries

A fresh, ripe strawberry is the taste of summer. Strawberry plants generally have a low, spreading growth suitable for large outdoor patches. If you have limited space outside, don't give up the dream of growing your berries. It is possible to get a good strawberry harvest indoors. You need to choose the right variety and give it what it needs to thrive, and you can have one or even two batches of berries per year.

Best indoor varieties

Almost any variety of strawberry can adapt to indoor conditions, but most throw out runners. They spread over a large area of ground, making containing a strawberry plant inside a little challenging. Alpine varieties of strawberries clump as they grow, so they take well to containers.

> **Strawberry Planting Tip**
>
> Bare-root strawberry plants are also known as runners. Before you plant a runner, be sure to soak it for 10 minutes.

Also, look for a cultivar that is everbearing to get more fruit. June-bearing strawberries produce fruit just once per year. Everbearing varieties produce two or more harvests. If you have low winter light in your home, try 'Camino Real,' a cultivar that will tolerate lower light conditions.

Light and heat

Ideal temperatures for strawberries are between about 68 and 77 degrees Fahrenheit. They will tolerate some variation, but ordinary room temperature should be fine. Just be careful about cold drafts. This is especially important if you place berries near windows to get light. A little insulating plastic or bubble wrap around the container can help keep the plant warm.

For light, direct, natural sunlight is best (BL 1,2,3). If you cannot provide your indoor strawberries with at least six hours of bright natural light, get a grow light to supplement. If you are only using a grow light, set it for 12 hours per day.

Watering

Before the first fruit emerges, your strawberry plant needs watering every day. Make sure the container has good drainage, though, so the roots do not get soggy. Once production begins, reduce watering to whenever you feel that the top inch of soil is dry. Established strawberry plants prefer an occasional, deep watering as opposed to regular, light watering.

Feeding

Ideal soil conditions for strawberries are slightly acidic and rich in organic material. To get a good yield of berries, fertilize about once a month with a well-balanced organic product. You can also use a controlled-release fertilizer just once. Check with your local garden center for a product specific to berries.

Harvesting

One of the great things about a strawberry harvest is that it is continuous. The berries do not ripen all at once, so you can enjoy picking and using them as they're ready. You'll know when the berries are ripe and ready to be harvested when they are bright red and just slightly soft. Taste one to know for sure. It should be sweet and juicy.

Troubleshooting

Strawberries are pretty forgiving, even when grown indoors and in containers. There are just a few issues you may encounter:

- **Tip burn.** If the strawberry leaves' tips look brown, dry, or burned, you may have a calcium deficiency. You could do a soil test or find a fertilizer with extra calcium.

- **Pests.** Indoor plants are not likely to get infested, but you may see aphids or spider mites, little insects on the leaves and stems. Use a soap and water spray to control them naturally.

- **Fungal infections.** Fungus thrives in warm, humid conditions. While strawberries are vulnerable to these infections, they are highly unlikely in the cooler, dry air indoors, especially in winter. If you do see mold or fungus, your plants may need more spacing for airflow. A fungicide may help, but depending on the extent of the infection, it may be easier to destroy the plant and start over.

Using

Most strawberry lovers will agree that the best way to use strawberries is fresh. The sweet, juicy flavor and texture of a homegrown, perfectly ripe strawberry is hard to beat. There are nearly endless uses for strawberries in the kitchen:

- In desserts, like fruit pies, crumbles, cakes, ice cream, and cookies

- Throw them in smoothies and mix into yogurt

- Use in cocktails

- Put slices in salads or make a vinaigrette

- Make strawberry fruit leather

Preserving

If you end up with more strawberries than you can eat fresh, try preserving them. Strawberry jam is a popular choice and is easy to make. You can also freeze them. Spread the strawberries out on a tray to freeze so that they do not stick together, and then store them in a freezer bag.

PROJECT #24:
STRAWBERRY FOUNTAIN

Skill level: Easy
Cost: $$
Power tools: No
Plants: Strawberry plant
Growing zones: BL 1,2,3
Supplemental light: Full-spectrum light if not enough direct sunlight

Growing strawberries indoors has never been so fun. There is lots of room for variation in this cute tabletop grower project that makes a fantastic living centerpiece.

WHAT YOU NEED

- large bowl - I chose an antique bowl for my project
- 3-inch piece of food-grade pipe, 10 inches long
- potting mix
- decorative rocks
- strawberry plant
- plastic spray paint, any color
- drill and 5/16th-inch drill bit

HOW TO MAKE IT

1   Use spray paint to color your pipe; let it dry thoroughly.

2   Drill four drainage holes near the bottom of the pipe.

3   Set the pipe in the center of the bowl, upright

4   Surround the pipe with decorative rocks - this will also hold the pipe in place.

5   Fill the pipe about halfway full with potting mix and plant the strawberry. Fill the rest of the pipe up with potting mix and water well.

6   Place in a sunny location and keep the soil in the pipe moist.

Figs

Fig trees are native to warm climates, but anyone can enjoy the fresh fruit by growing figs indoors. Unlike many other fruit trees, figs mature quickly, and fruit develops in the first one or two years. It's a good return on investment. Along with the fruit for your kitchen, an indoor fig is a lovely plant that lends a tropical feel to the indoor environment.

Few fruits are more sweet or delicious than fresh figs. If you never thought you could grow a fig because of your climate, follow these guidelines to enjoy a beautiful, fruiting tree indoors.

Best indoors varieties

In their natural environments, fig trees grow large. Select a smaller variety or even a dwarf type. You can also manage size by keeping the tree in a pot that confines the roots and regularly pruning offshoots. Another important consideration for indoor growing is fruit. Avoid the ornamental varieties, which do not bear edible fruit.
These are some of the best fig varieties for indoor growing:

- **Little Ruby** - This fig variety has a semi-compact growth habit, making it perfect for an indoor edible garden. It is also prized for its tasty, reddish-brown figs with a ruby center.

- **Black Jack** - This attractive semi-dwarf fig tree produces super sweet and elongated purple fruit.

- **Negro Largo** - This small cultivar is also known as Brown Turkey. It produces medium-sized fruit, and is especially tolerant of heavy pruning.

Light and heat

Fig trees require a minimum of six hours of bright light per day. A south-facing window is best (BL 1,2). If you don't think that your tree is getting enough light through windows, use a grow light as a supplement. The more light you can provide, the more fruit you'll get.

The minimum temperatures for a fig tree are between 50 and 54 degrees Fahrenheit. Do not let them get cooler than this. Make sure you place the tree away from cold doorway drafts. If the window near the tree is drafty, put up plastic insulation during the coldest months to allow your tree to get sunlight and stay warm.

Watering

Make sure the container for the fig drains well and use a lighter soil mix for added drainage. The soil should be moist but not soggy most of the time. Water whenever you can feel that the first inch of soil in the pot is dry.

Figs prefer humidity, and many indoor environments are dry, especially in winter. Mist your fig tree's leaves daily or provide humidity with a pebble tray. Fill a shallow tray with pebbles and water and set the pot on top of it. This will provide a local area of humid air around the tree.

Feeding

Getting the right balance of fertilizer is essential for a healthy fig tree that produces fruit. Too little nutrition and the tree will not thrive, too much, and it will put energy into leaves instead of fruit. Figs respond best to liquid or slow-release balanced fertilizers applied in spring and as new growth begins and again in mid-summer.

Harvesting

Figs ripen as they change from green to purple or brown. Also, look at how the fruit hangs to determine harvest time. The figs should hang downward as they ripen. Even varieties that do not change color will hang down when it's time to pick them, so this is a great way to tell if they're ready.

Troubleshooting

Your fig tree should grow well indoors, but you may encounter a few problems:

- **Yellowing leaves, leaf drop.** These signs on the leaves typically indicate inadequate light. Try a grow light if you are already placing the fig at your sunniest window.

- **Low or no fruit production.** Too much or too little water is a common cause of inadequate fruit production. During hot weather and dry conditions, water more often. To avoid overwatering, let the soil dry a little between soakings. Another issue could be too much nitrogen fertilizer. Reduce nitrogen or add more phosphorus during feedings.

- **Brown spots on leaves.** Fig trees can be susceptible to fig rust, a fungal infection usually caused by overwatering and too much humidity. A fungicide may help.

Enjoying figs

With a harvest of figs, you need some recipes and ideas for using them in the kitchen. Thankfully, you can use this versatile fruit in many ways:

Enjoy fresh figs with blue cheese.

- Add figs to salads.

- Make a fig syrup for cocktails.

- A fresh fig tart is a delicious way to use up several fruits.

- Grill figs for dessert and eat with honey and cheese.

- Try poached figs in port wine.

- Use in sauces for all kinds of meat dishes.

Fig Facts

Fig puree can be used in place of fat in baked goods and will help keep your baked goods moist

Preserving figs

Fresh figs have a short shelf life. Enjoy them as soon as you can and store them for just a week or so fresh in the refrigerator. Preserve the fruits you can't eat fresh:

- To freeze, arrange the figs on a tray and put them in the freezer. When frozen, put them in a bag to store.

- Use a dehydrator to dry figs. Dry the figs whole or cut in half.

- Try canning figs to preserve them. Make a jam or pickle the fruit for extended shelf life.

Project #25:
Fresh Figs Caramelized

Have a harvest of figs and arc looking for something new to do with them? Figs are among the sweetest and tastiest of fruits, delicious both raw and cooked. To enhance the sugar and rich flavor of your figs, try carmelizing them. It's a simple, fast recipe.

WHAT YOU NEED

- About a dozen figs cut in half, lengthwise
- ½ cup of sugar
- ¼ teaspoon of salt
- ¼ cup of balsamic vinegar or a fortified wine like port
- 1 ½ tablespoon unsalted butter
- 1 teaspoon lemon juice, preferably fresh

HOW TO MAKE IT

1   Mix the sugar and salt in a dish and press each fig half into it. Make sure you coat the cut-side of the fig well with the sugar and salt mixture.

2   Place each fig half, cut-side down, into a hot skillet over high heat. Cook them for a few minutes. Look for golden brown caramelization. As each one is ready, turn it over so the cut-side is facing up.

3   Remove from heat and add the balsamic vinegar or wine to the skillet. Put the skillet back on the heat for 30 seconds or a minute, just to reduce the liquid. Scrape up crystallized bits of fruit and sugar as it thickens.

4   Take the pan off the heat again and add the butter and lemon juice. Stir to combine. Your caramelized figs are ready to enjoy once they have cooled a little bit.

Master Tip: Caramelized figs are delicious alone for a dessert or snack, but they really shine as an ice cream topping. Eat them on top of French toast or waffles for breakfast or plain yogurt for a healthier option.

Nectarines

Nectarines taste like summer. There's nothing like the sweet, juicy, peach flavor—without the disconcerting fuzzy skin—on a warm summer day. Nectarines are versatile too. They taste fantastic when fresh and perfectly ripe but can also be grilled, baked, and used in savory and sweet recipes.

You don't need an orchard or the perfect climate to grow nectarines. A dwarf variety will grow well in a container right in your home. Ensure it receives the right conditions, and your nectarine tree will provide a delicious, annual harvest.

Best indoor varieties

A standard nectarine tree is not a small tree, so choose a dwarf variety well suited to container growing. You won't have to worry about transplanting or pruning to manage size. These are some of the best varieties that should thrive indoors:

- **Dwarf Flavortop** - This self-pollinating semi-dwarf tree produces sweet and tangy firm fruit with reddish-orange skin and yellow flesh. This small tree reaches about 8 feet tall at maturity.

- **Necta Zee Miniature** - This self-pollinating, moderate winter chill dwarf tree only reaches 6 feet at maturity, making it perfect for containers. It produces sweet, yellow-fleshed semi-cling fruit.

- **Dwarf Nectar Babe** - This miniature nectarine tree produces a hearty crop of sweet, yellow-fleshed freestone fruit. Reaching up to 6 feet at maturity, this nectarine tree is perfect for an indoor edible garden. You will need another nectarine or peachtree for pollination.

For a white-fleshed nectarine, try 'Arctic Babe' or 'Arctic Sprite.' Some varieties come in both standard size and a dwarf or miniature version. Make sure you purchase a smaller tree for indoor growing.

Light and heat

A nectarine tree needs a minimum of six hours of bright light per day to be healthy and produce fruit. Choose a south-facing window and consider moving the pot outdoors in summer to catch more natural light (BL 1,2,3). If window light is hard to come by in the winter, get a grow light.

Once a nectarine has achieved its chill hours for the winter, it will do just fine indoors at room temperature. Avoid cold drafts and dry, hot air from heating vents when you place the container inside.

Nectarines Need Chilling Time

When choosing a nectarine variety, you must also consider chill hours. This is the number of hours the plant must be in conditions under 45 degrees Fahrenheit in the dormant season to produce fruit. Like nectarines, fruits that grow in moderate climates have a chill hour rating in the few hundreds.

Look for a variety with a lower number and plan to keep your tree outside for this period in the fall before it freezes.

Watering

Your tree needs regular watering to keep the soil moist but not dripping wet. Start with a suitable container that has an adequate number of drainage holes. Use a potting mix with some organic matter to add nutrients and to improve drainage.

Water more often in the summer. To check when your nectarine needs another watering, put your finger in the soil. If it is dry down to two inches, it's time to water again.

Feeding

Fertilizer is particularly crucial for potted plants with limited root reach and soil nutrients. A healthy nectarine tree in a container needs fertilizer in the spring before fruiting. Another dose in late summer is also a good idea. Choose a fertilizer with a little more phosphorus and not too much nitrogen. Products designed for citrus trees work well for nectarine trees.

Harvesting

Your nectarines will be ready to pick over a few weeks, not all at once. Rely on signs that the fruit is ready rather than a particular time for harvesting. The color of a ripe nectarine is yellow with a red blush and no green. You should get a good whiff of nectarine smell when it's ready for picking, and it should give a little when squeezed.

Troubleshooting

If you have issues with your nectarine tree, it should be easy to fix as long as you act quickly. Don't let problems go too far before looking for a solution, or the tree could die.

- **Low or no fruit production.** A fruit tree that has stopped producing may be getting too little or too much water. Never let the soil dry out completely, or the roots stand in water. A fertilizer with too much nitrogen can also cause this problem.

- **Brown edges on leaves.** This can indicate that you are overfertilizing your tree. Dilute the fertilizer and use it less often.

- **Curling leaves, brown spots on fruit.** These are signs of fungal infections known to infest nectarine trees. It's less likely your indoor tree will be vulnerable, but if you see these signs, you may need a fungicide to save it.

Can I Start a Nectarine from Seed?

If you wish to grow a nectarine from a pit, the first thing you need to know is that it can take 3-4 years for it to bear fruit. With that said, it can be done and is a fun project for those who are patient.

- Once you have a pit, scrub off any remaining fruit with a brush or sponge and some water. Let the pit dry for 24 hours.

- Use a nutcracker or a hammer to carefully get the seed out.

- Place the seed in a cup of water for 24 hours. If it sinks it is good to use. If it floats it is a dud.

- Wrap a viable seed in a damp paper towel and put it in a sealable plastic bag. Place it somewhere warm and keep it moist.

- When the roots are about two inches long it is time to plant.

- Enjoy your tree as a beautiful houseplant for a few years until it is ready to produce fruit.

Using

The best thing you can do with a nectarine from your tree is to eat it fresh. The good thing about having a tree is that you can enjoy a harvest big enough to do so much more with this delicious summer fruit:

- Add slices of nectarines to salads
- Grill nectarine halves and eat with vanilla ice cream
- Make a nectarine crisp
- Cook with meats for a sweet and savory sauce
- Make a stone fruit pie

Preserving

If you ate canned peaches in syrup as a child, you know what a great treat it is. You can do the same with nectarines. Can your fruit to enjoy as a sweet treat in winter. There is also another way to preserve nectarines if you are looking for an effort-free option: freeze them. Cut into slices and freeze on a tray, then store in a sealable bag.

Growing nectarines is not as hard as it sounds. If your space is limited, grow a dwarf tree in a container, and enjoy a tasty, yearly harvest of this gorgeous fruit.

PROJECT #26:
GOOD MORNING
NECTARINE SMOOTHIE

Skill level: Easy
Cost: $
Plants: Nectarines
Use: Great way to get your morning started

This protein-packed smoothie gives you just the right amount of energy to get your day off to a great start. Following these measurements will make just enough for you and your best friend to enjoy.

WHAT YOU NEED

- 2 medium nectarines, pitted and cut in quarters
- ½ cup unsweetened almond milk
- 1 tablespoon raw honey
- ⅓ cup plain Greek yogurt
- ¼ cup vanilla whey protein powder
- ice

HOW TO MAKE IT

1 Combine all ingredients in a blender and blend well.

Master Tip: Add a handful of spinach or kale to this delicious drink for a powerful nutritional boost.

Pineapple Guava

Did you know that pineapple guava is not true guava? It's still a worthwhile ornamental and fruit-bearing tree to grow, even indoors. Also known as guavasteen, it produces a sweet fruit reminiscent of apple, mint, and pineapple.

Pineapple guava is an easy fruit to grow compared to many others. It grows up to 15 feet tall in the garden but can be smaller and shrubbier when grown in a pot. Enjoy a harvest of this unique fruit as well as the pretty evergreen leaves and spring flowers.

Best indoor varieties

Compared to true guavas, pineapple guava grows well indoors and in containers. It is not a large tree, and it takes well to pruning that keeps it smaller and shrubbier. For the best fruit production, pick these cultivars:

- **Andre -** This self-fertile variety is from Brazil and produces large, oblong to round fruit with a rich flavor.

- **Coolidge -** This self-fertile variety grows a hardy crop of large, dark green, delicious fruit.

- **Ruby -** This self-fertile variety of pineapple guava grows to about six feet tall. It is a heavy producer, with round to pear-shaped fruit the size of a baseball.

Light and heat

Pineapple guava does not like extreme heat or extreme cold, although it will tolerate some of each. Avoid spots indoors with cold or warm drafts of dry air, such as near a door or heating vent. To produce fruit, pineapple guava needs 50 chill hours spent at about 43 degrees Fahrenheit or less. Place it in a cool spot (such as by a door) for a few days each winter.

Outside, pineapple guava prefers full sun but tolerates partial shade. For your indoor plant, put it near a southern window (BL 1,2), and it should get enough light. Six hours per day is adequate.

Watering

Drainage is essential to avoid soggy, rotting roots on your pineapple guava. Make sure the container drains well and that the soil mix you choose is not too heavy. Water needs are moderate. Aim for soil that is consistently damp and not soaking wet. Water less in the winter, but don't let the soil dry out entirely.

Feeding

One of the reasons that pineapple guava is well suited to containers is that it grows slowly. This also means it does not need a lot of fertilizer. Use a slow-release, balanced fertilizer just once or twice per year to get good fruit production. It also helps to start with a high-quality potting soil enriched with compost or other organic matter.

Harvesting

Pineapple guava also makes harvesting easy. The fruit naturally drops from the tree when ready. This is especially helpful because it does not change color with ripeness. The fruits remain green.

When it drops from the tree, your pineapple guava fruit may be a little firm still. This protects it from bruising and means you may want to leave it out for a few days for perfect ripeness. The fruit should feel just slightly soft when pressed.

Troubleshooting

If your pineapple guava is not producing fruit, there could be several reasons:

- A grafted or seed-grown pineapple guava will not produce fruit for about three years, so be patient with younger trees.

- Both extremes of hot and cold can limit fruit production.

- Your tree may not be getting enough light. It should get six hours per day of direct sunlight at a minimum.

- You may be overwatering the tree. Pineapple guava needs moist soil that is not soggy. Check to be sure your container drains properly.

- Another issue you may see is yellowing leaves. This may indicate that the soil is too alkaline. Try adding peat moss to the soil, which will both lower the pH and improve drainage.

Using

The flavor of pineapple guava is spectacular. Enjoy the fruit fresh by cutting it in half and scooping out the insides. You can also eat the flowers, although you'll get no fruit if you use them all. Enjoy the fresh flowers in salads or iced tea and cocktails.

Ripe guava should be enjoyed within a few days, although you can refrigerate it to extend its shelf life to a week or two. By two weeks, it will be overripe and unusable. In addition to eating it fresh, try pineapple guava:

- In a smoothie
- On top of homemade ice cream or yogurt
- In dessert breads or pancakes
- Baked with chicken
- In cocktails

Preserving

To keep extra fruit from your pineapple guava, try preserving it in a jam. It makes delicious fruit preserves with a little lemon juice and sugar. Jam is the best way to preserve pineapple guava, but you can freeze the fruit as an alternative. Peel first and let it freeze on a tray before storing it in a freezer bag.

Project #27: Pineapple Guava Perfect Pie

Skill level: Easy
Cost: $
Plants: Pineapple guava
Use: Great way to get your morning started

This naturally sweet pie makes the perfect dessert. Pair with homemade ice cream for a fabulous end to any meal.

WHAT YOU NEED

- 2 tablespoons all-purpose gluten-free flour
- ½ cup white sugar
- 1 lime, zested
- 1 teaspoon ground cinnamon
- ¼ teaspoon ground nutmeg
- ⅛ teaspoon salt
- 9-inch gluten-free double-crust pie shell
- 4 cups peeled, seeded, and thinly sliced guava fruits
- 1 tablespoon lime juice
- 3 tablespoons cold butter, cut into small pieces

HOW TO MAKE IT

1   Preheat oven to 425 degrees F.

2   Add flour, sugar, lime zest, cinnamon, nutmeg, and salt to a mixing bowl and combine.

3   Place the pie crust in a 9-inch pie plate.

4   Place the guava slices on the bottom of the crust, mounding them towards the center of the crust.

5   Sprinkle the flour and sugar mixture on the guava. Drizzle the filling with the lime juice and place the butter pieces on top.

6   Place the second pie crust on top and crimp the edges together.

7   Slit the top in several places to allow the steam to escape.

8   Bake for 10 minutes, then reduce the temperature to 350 degrees and bake until the crust is golden for about 30 to 40 minutes.

Master Tip: Rather than a pie crust top, try a crumble topping made with brown sugar, flour, and butter.

SOWING THINGS UP

The next time someone tells you that you can't have an indoor edible garden all year long - show them the proof! You can be a successful indoor gardener and produce a sizable harvest to enjoy 365 days a year. So, let the wind blow and the snow fly; things will be green in your home no matter the weather!

I truly hope that you have enjoyed reading this book as much as I have enjoyed writing it. Embrace your indoor gardening journey, and remember: you are not limited by your space, the weather, or your experiences. Growing food is a great thing. Growing food all year is even better!

Happy Growing,

Susan Patterson, CBHC, Master Gardener, and Author

P.S. If you need assistance or have garden questions or just want to chat about all things garden, feel feel free to email me: **Susan@backyardvitality.com.**

> "If you've never experienced the joy of accomplishing more than you can imagine, plant a garden. "
>
> *- Robert Breault*

BEST INDOOR EDIBLE PLANTS

Here is a list of some of the best edible plants to grow indoors.

Herbs and Flowers

Plant	Suggested Growing Zones
Basil	BL 1,2,3
Calendula	BL 1, 2, 3
Chives	BL 1,2,3
Cilantro	BL 2, 3
Dendrobium orchid	BL 2, 3
Dill	BL 1, 2
Lemon Balm	BL 1, 2, 3 & PL 1
Lemongrass	BL 1, 2, 3
Mint	BL 2, 3
Mum	BL 2,3 & PL 1
Nasturtium	BL 1, 2
Oregano	BL 1, 2, 3
Parsley	BL 1, 2
Rosemary	BL 1, 2, 3
Sage	BL 1, 2, 3
Scented geranium	BL 1, 2, 3
Tulip	BL 2, PL 2
Thyme	BL 1, 2, 3
Viola	BL 1, 2, 3

Sprouts, Roots, and Greens

Plant	Suggested Growing Zones
Beets	BL 2
Bok choi	BL 2 & PL 1, 2
Carrots	BL 2 & PL 2
Garlic greens	BL 1, 2, 3
Ginger root	BL 1,2
Kale	BL 1,2,3
Lettuce	BL 2 & PL 1, 2
Microgreens	BL 1, 2, 3 & PL 1
Mushrooms	BL 2 & PL 1, 2
Radish	BL 2, 3 & PL 1
Scallions	BL 1,2,3
Spinach	BL 2, 3 & PL 1
Sprouts	BL 2, 3, & PL 1,2
Wheatgrass	BL 1, 2 & PL, 1,2

Other FoxTrot Books by Bill Amend

FoxTrot
Pass the Loot
Black Bart Says Draw
Eight Yards, Down and Out
Bury My Heart at Fun-Fun Mountain
Say Hello to Cactus Flats
May the Force Be With Us, Please
Take Us to Your Mall
The Return of the Lone Iguana
At Least This Place Sells T-Shirts
Come Closer, Roger, There's a Mosquito on Your Nose
Welcome to Jasorassic Park

Anthologies

FoxTrot: The Works
FoxTrot *en masse*
Enormously FoxTrot
Wildly FoxTrot
FoxTrot Beyond a Doubt
Camp FoxTrot

I'm Flying, Jack
...I Mean, Roger

**A FoxTrot Collection
by Bill Amend**

**Andrews McMeel
Publishing**

Kansas City

9

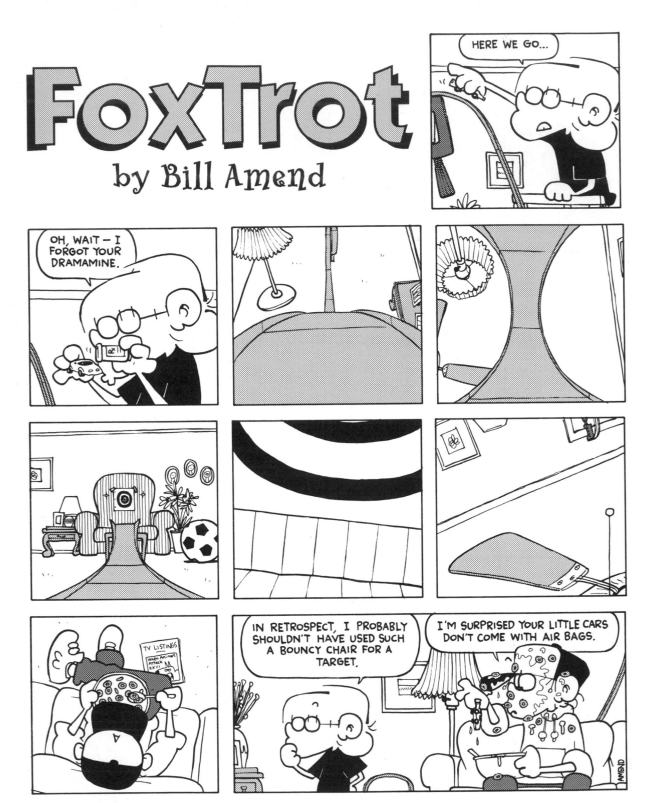

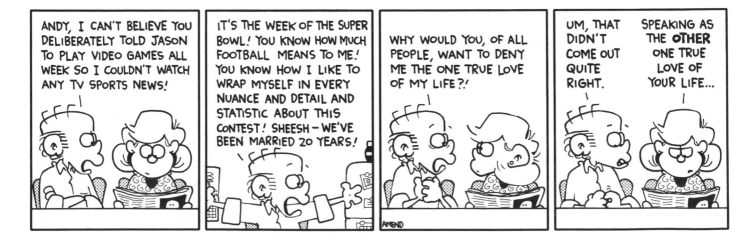

12

FoxTrot
by Bill Amend

MAYBE IF I EAT A BREATH MINT...

MOM, CAN I HAVE A POP-TART BEFORE DINNER?

MOM, CAN I HAVE A—...

HOLD ON A SEC...

JASON, I'M ON THE TELEPHONE!

CLICK MOM, CAN I HAVE A POP-TART BEFORE DINNER?

I MEANT WAIT UNTIL I'M DONE, JASON.

class. I will not shoot rubber bands in class. I will not shoot rubber bands in class. I will not shoot rubber bands in class. I will not shoot rubber bands in class. I will not shoot rubber bands in class. I will not shoot rubber bands in class. I will

fake vomit in the cafeteria. I will not put in the cafeteria.

throw paper airplanes will not throw paper airplanes assembly. I will not throw during assembly. I will not paper airplanes during assembly. I paper airplanes during assem paper airplanes

UM, JASON? ASSEMBLY'S NOT UNTIL TOMORROW.

I KNOW, BUT I HAVE A DENTIST APPOINTMENT AFTER SCHOOL.

YOU KNOW, MOM, ACCORDING TO MY CINEGEEK MAGAZINE, THEY USED A 44-FOOT MODEL FOR A LOT OF THOSE SHOTS OF THE TITANIC.

AND AT THE END? WHERE EVERYONE'S SUPPOSEDLY FREEZING IN THE OCEAN? THEY FILMED IT IN A HEATED INDOOR POOL AND ADDED ALL THE FOGGY BREATH WITH COMPUTERS.

IN FACT, FOR THIS ONE SCENE WITH JACK AND ROSE RUNNING AWAY FROM A WALL OF WATER...

JASON, ARE YOU **TRYING** TO SABOTAGE MY LOVE OF THE MOVIE?!

DAD, IF SHE'S FIGURED OUT YOUR PLAN, DO I STILL GET PAID?

WELL, I'M OFF TO THE 6:00 SCREENING. THE TV DINNERS ARE WHERE THEY WERE LAST NIGHT.

SWEETHEART, DON'T YOU THINK YOU MIGHT BE GETTING JUST A LITTLE CARRIED AWAY?

YOU'VE SEEN "TITANIC" *HOW* MANY TIMES NOW? TWENTY-FOUR?

WATCHING IT OVER AND OVER ISN'T GOING TO CHANGE THE ENDING... THE BOAT **SINKS**! IT'S SAD, BUT WHAT'S DONE IS DONE!

I KNOW, BUT AT LEAST WHILE I'M IN THE THEATER, IT'S LIKE EVERYONE'S STILL ALIVE FOR THOSE SIX HOURS.

UM, DON'T YOU MEAN THREE HOURS?

I CAN'T DRIVE ALL THE WAY TO THE CINEPLEX AND JUST SEE IT ONCE.

ROGER, I KNOW IT MUST SEEM WEIRD THAT I'VE GONE SO GOO-GOO OVER "TITANIC."

BUT SOMETHING ABOUT THAT FILM HAS RESONATED WITH ME LIKE NOTHING HAS IN WHO KNOWS HOW LONG.

IT'S MADE ME WANT TO LIVE! TO LOVE! TO MAKE EACH DAY COUNT! TO GET OUT AND **DO** THINGS!

LIKE WHAT?

I'M FLYING, JACK! ... I MEAN, ROGER.

ACTUALLY, I'D RATHER YOU **DIDN'T** USE MY REAL NAME RIGHT NOW.

19

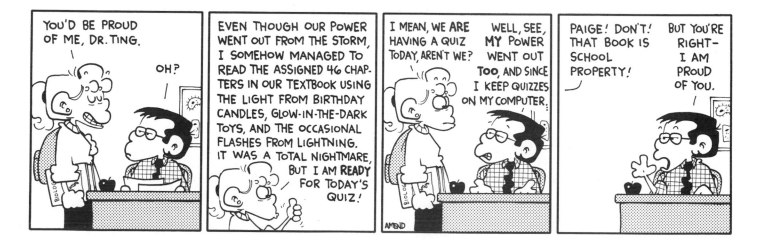

Panel 1: NOW THEN, JASON, WHERE WERE WE BEFORE WE WERE DISTRACTED BY ALL OF THE RAIN AND FLOODING LAST WEEK?

Panel 2: OH, THAT'S RIGHT... YOU HAD JUST LET SLIP THE ADMISSION THAT YOU REALLY DO LIKE ME. SHALL WE PICK UP WHERE WE LEFT OFF?

Panel 4: WHAM! WHAM! WHAM! WHAM! | ACTUALLY, I THINK YOU WERE BEATING YOUR HEAD ON THIS LOCKER OVER HERE.

Panel 5: "TIME TRAVEL: FACT AND FICTION."

Panel 6: "WORM HOLES AND TIME PORTALS: DO THEY EXIST?"

Panel 7: "REVERSING TIME: A PHYSICIST'S GUIDE."

Panel 8: I ALWAYS WONDERED WHAT WOULD HAPPEN THE DAY YOU ADMITTED TO LIKING A GIRL. | I'M GONNA BEAT THIS THING. YOU WATCH.

Panel 9: *TIME TRAVEL?!?* ARE YOU INSANE?? | IT'S THE PERFECT SOLUTION TO MY PREDICAMENT, PETER.

Panel 10: I FIGURE OUT A WAY TO GO BACK A WEEK, WARN MYSELF ABOUT EILEEN JACOBSON'S LITTLE SCHEME, AND IN DOING SO, PREVENT MYSELF FROM MAKING THE BIGGEST GAFFE OF MY LIFE!

Panel 11: WHAT COULD BE SIMPLER?

Panel 12: WELL, THE TERM "EVERYTHING" LEAPS TO MIND. | LET'S SEE... I GUESS I SHOULD START BY DEBUNKING EINSTEIN...

Panel 1:
JASON, YOU HAVEN'T TOUCHED YOUR DINNER AT ALL! SORRY, MOM. I'M ON A SUPER CRASH DIET.

Panel 2:
WHAT?? YOU'RE NOTHING BUT SKIN AND BONES AS IT IS! I KNOW, BUT IF I WANT TO TRAVEL BACK IN TIME, I NEED TO GET MY BODY'S REST MASS DOWN TO ABSOLUTE ZERO SO THAT I CAN EXCEED THE SPEED OF LIGHT.

Panel 3:
IT'S A PAIN, BUT THAT STUFF I TOLD EILEEN JACOBSON LAST WEEK HAS GOT TO BE UNDONE.

Panel 4:
SO THIS CRASH DIET HAS NOTHING TO DO WITH MY SERVING EGGPLANT LOAF TONIGHT? TOTALLY A COINCIDENCE. BUT I APPRECIATE THE HELP.

Panel 5:
PETER, I'M GOING TO NEED YOUR HELP. WITH WHAT?

Panel 6:
AS YOU KNOW, I'VE BEEN PURSUING TIME TRAVEL AS THE SOLUTION TO MY RECENT EILEEN JACOBSON PROBLEM.

$L' = L \sqrt{1 - \frac{v^2}{c^2}}$

Panel 7:
WELL, IF MY THEORIES ON THE SUBJECT ARE CORRECT, I'M GOING TO NEED TO EXCEED THE SPEED OF LIGHT, WHICH IS ROUGHLY 670 MILLION MPH. MOST PHYSICISTS SAY IT'S IMPOSSIBLE, BUT I SAY IT CAN BE DONE. WHERE DO I COME IN?

Panel 8:
I'VE SEEN HOW YOU DRIVE ON THE FREEWAY. YOU'RE TALKING NINE-DIGIT SPEEDS. I'VE ONLY FLIRTED WITH **FOUR**.

Panel 9:
WELL, EILEEN, YOU'VE LUCKED OUT. OH?

Panel 10:
I SPENT THIS ENTIRE WEEK RESEARCHING TIME TRAVEL SO THAT I COULD GO BACK AND STOP MYSELF FROM EVER SAYING THAT I LIKED YOU, BUT I'VE CONCLUDED IT CAN'T BE DONE.

Panel 11:
AND BELIEVE ME, I WORKED HARDER ON THIS THAN I'VE WORKED ON ANYTHING IN MY LIFE. DAY AND NIGHT, NIGHT AND DAY, SEARCHING, PRAYING, AGONIZING FOR THE SOLUTION THAT WOULD GET ME **OUT** OF THIS BIND. BUT, ALAS, A HAPPY ENDING WASN'T TO BE.

Panel 12:
SO... LOOKS LIKE I'M YOUR BEAU. AND... I'VE LUCKED OUT **HOW** EXACTLY?

I CAN ALWAYS TELL THE MORNINGS WHEN YOU HAVE A MATH TEST SCHEDULED. I MADE THE COFFEE EXTRA-STRONG. I HOPE YOU DON'T MIND.

ROGER, YOU DIDN'T EAT BREAKFAST!

NO TIME, SWEETIE — I'M GOING TO BE LATE.

PAIGE, YOU DIDN'T EAT BREAKFAST!

NO TIME, MOTHER — I'M GOING TO BE LATE.

JASON, YOU DIDN'T EAT BREAKFAST!

NO TIME, MOM — I'M GOING TO BE LATE.

THINK OF ME AS AN ISLAND IN A SEA OF SCREWY PRIORITIES.

EXCEPT THAT YOU NEEDED TO BE SOMEWHERE AN HOUR AGO.

KIDS? WHAT DO YOU WANT FOR DINNER TONIGHT?

TAKE-OUT PIZZA!
TAKE-OUT CHINESE!
TAKE-OUT MEXICAN!
TAKE-OUT BARBECUE!
TAKE-OUT SUSHI!
TAKE-OUT BURGERS!
TAKE-OUT CHICKEN!

LET ME REPHRASE THAT... WHAT DO YOU WANT ME TO **MAKE** FOR DINNER?

KIDS?

LOOK AT IT THIS WAY, SWEETIE — A LOT OF COOKS WORK THEIR WHOLE **LIVES** TRYING TO EARN A REPUTATION. THANK YOU, MR. PICK-ME-UP.

MOM? DO TV DINNERS COUNT?

FoxTrot
by Bill Amend

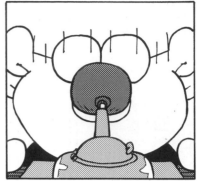

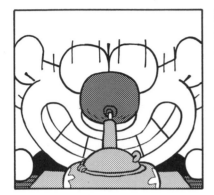

I REALLY SHOULD'VE SPRUNG FOR THE RADIO-CONTROLLED MODEL.

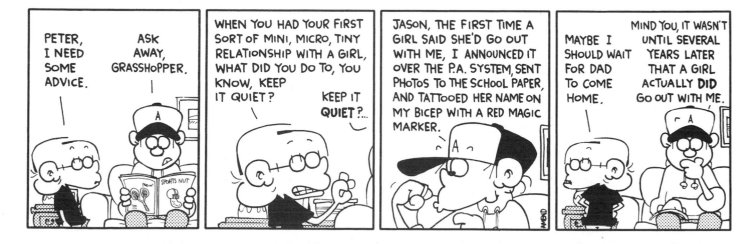

36

38

41

MARCUS, JASON HAS SOMETHING HE WANTS TO TELL YOU.

I DO?! HEH HEH... ER... WELL... I GUESS I DO... ER...

BASICALLY, MARCUS... UM... WHAT YOU... ER... AS MY BEST FRIEND.. UM... SHOULD KNOW... UM... IS THAT EILEEN AND I... HEH HEH... KINDA L—... L—...

AAAGH! I CAN'T DO IT!

DON'T TELL ME YOU TWO ARE LIKE AN ITEM OR SOMETHING.

NOT AS OF RIGHT NOW.

JASON, DEAR, THOSE WINDOWS DON'T OPEN.

EILEEN, C'MON! YOU'VE GOT TO GIVE ME A SECOND CHANCE!

RIGHT.

I'M NEW AT THIS "LIKING GIRLS" STUFF! I'M BOUND TO STUMBLE A LITTLE! I'LL TELL MARCUS THE NEXT OPPORTUNITY I GET! I SWEAR! CROSS MY HEART!

TELL ME WHAT?

MARCUS! UM... WELL... ER... GULP...

EILEEN, C'MON! YOU'VE GOT TO GIVE ME A THIRD CHANCE!

WRONG.

SO... HOW ARE THINGS GOING WITH YOUR LITTLE GAL PAL?

CAN YOU SAY "TOTAL NUCLEAR MELTDOWN"?

UH-OH. WHAT HAPPENED?

THIS WHOLE YEAR IT'S BEEN OBVIOUS THAT EILEEN HAS WANTED ME TO LIKE HER, BUT AS SOON AS I TOLD HER I DID, I DISCOVERED SHE HAD ALL THESE RIDICULOUS EXPECTATIONS AND CONDITIONS ATTACHED!

SUCH AS?

WELL, FOR STARTERS, SHE WANTED ME TO ACTUALLY ACT AS THOUGH I LIKED HER!

THIS NUCLEAR MELTDOWN... WAS IT PERCHANCE IN YOUR BRAIN?

OH, WELL. BETTER TO FIND THESE THINGS OUT NOW THAN AFTER WE'D GOTTEN ENGAGED OR SOMETHING, I GUESS.

46

Panel 1: FAVORITE MOTHER... WONDERFUL MOTHER... BEAUTIFUL MOTHER...

Panel 2: FLAWLESS AND WISE—

PAIGE, WITH A BUILD-UP LIKE THAT, I CAN PROMISE YOU IN ADVANCE, MY ANSWER IS "NO."

Panel 3: DO YOU MIND IF I PUT OFF MY HOMEWORK SO I CAN GO TO THE MALL?

Panel 4: I'LL BE HOME IN TIME FOR DINNER.

I'M OBVIOUSLY NOT **THAT** WISE.

FAVORITE MOTHER... WONDERFUL MOTHER...

Panel 5: OUR BROTHER IS SO WEIRD.

OH?

Panel 6: YOU KNOW HOW THE NIGHT BEFORE A MATH TEST, HE SLEEPS WITH HIS MATH BOOK UNDER HIS PILLOW?...

Panel 7: AND HE DOES THE SAME THING FOR TESTS IN ENGLISH, SCIENCE AND HISTORY?...

HE BELIEVES IN OSMOSIS. SO?

Panel 8: WELL, THEY'RE GIVING A BUNCH OF JUNIORS I.Q. TESTS TODAY.

SO **THAT'S** WHAT HAPPENED TO THE ENCYCLOPEDIA SET.

SCOOT OVER.

Panel 12: THAT'S H-O-R-S-E. I WIN.

GEE, WHAT A FUN GAME, MR. FIVE-HOOK-SHOTS-IN-A-ROW.

Panel 1: LET ME GET THIS STRAIGHT— YOU TAUGHT A TWO-YEAR-OLD TO SAY "☆@#☉"?! — I DIDN'T, PETER, THE STUPID JERZY SPANIEL SHOW DID!

Panel 2: ALL *I* DID WAS HAVE THE TV ON WHILE THE KID WAS PLAYING IN THE SAME ROOM!

Panel 3: I EVEN EXPLAINED TO HER THE PARENTAL WARNING AND TOLD HER NOT TO WATCH OR LISTEN!

Panel 4: GEE, I STAND CORRECTED, THEN. — I MEAN, WHAT AM I SUPPOSED TO DO — WATCH "BARNEY" THE WHOLE TIME I'M BABYSITTING?! / ☆@#☉ BARNEY! ☆@#☉ BARNEY!

Panel 5: THERE SHE IS! THERE'S MY WIDDLE DARLING!

Panel 6: DID YOU AND PAIGE HAVE FUN TODAY?! DID YOU READ LOTS OF BOOKS? DID YOU LEARN ANY NEW WORDS?

Panel 8: WHAT'S WITH THE SIX OPEN JARS OF PEANUT BUTTER? — WELL, IT'S TIME I MMPH. SHOULD BE GOING...

Panel 9: SO? WHAT HAPPENED WITH YOUR LITTLE CRISIS? — FORTUNATELY, MS. O'DELL REACTED REASONABLY WELL.

Panel 10: SHE SAID A TWO-YEAR-OLD IS BOUND TO REPEAT AN OCCASIONAL INAPPROPRIATE WORD NOW AND THEN, BUT SO LONG AS YOU DON'T REINFORCE IT OR LEND IT MEANING, THE KID'LL PROBABLY DROP IT WITH NO HARM DONE.

Panel 11: "REASONABLY WELL"?? IT SOUNDS LIKE SHE TOOK IT GREAT. — WELL, THEN WE GOT INTO MY WATCHING JERZY SPANIEL WHILE BABYSITTING.

Panel 12: I SEE. SO "REASONABLY WELL" DESCRIBES HER **AVERAGE** REACTION. — WANT A PENNY?

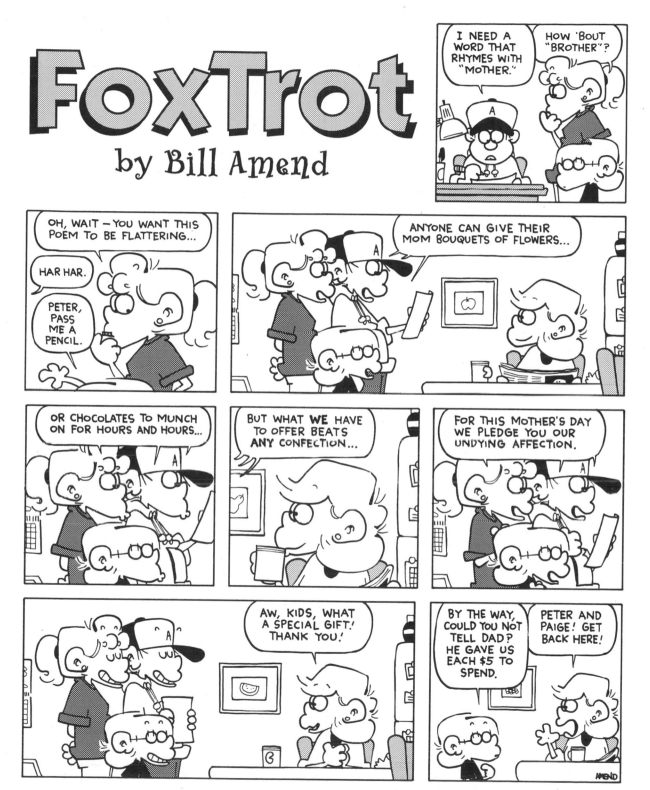

WHAT'S ON THE CAFETERIA MENU FOR TODAY? **I CAN'T MAKE IT OUT.**

SOMETHING MUST'VE GONE WRONG WITH THE COPIER— ALL THE WORDS ARE UN-RECOGNIZABLE BLOBS.

WELL, THAT'S NOT EXACTLY HELPFUL.

THEN AGAIN... **ACTUALLY, THE MENU'S BLOBS SEEMED MORE APPETIZING.** GLOP!

AMEND

ONE BOTTLE OF HOT SAUCE...

TWO BOTTLES OF HOT SAUCE... THREE BOTTLES OF HOT SAUCE...

AMEND

REMIND ME TO STOP SERVING TACOS ON DAYS YOU KIDS GO TO THE DENTIST. **IS NOVOCAINE GREAT, OR WHAT?!**

NICE UNIFORM. **THANKS.**

LET ME GUESS— CAUGHT STEALING? **BIG-TIME.**

AMEND

SECOND BASE? THIRD BASE? HOME? **KEEP GOING.**

ONE OF YOUR TEAMMATES' SUNFLOWER SEEDS? **I'M SORRY, BUT "RAGING BULL" TRUCKOWSKI HAS GOT TO LEARN TO SHARE!**

UGGH. I'M TOO FULL TO TAKE ANOTHER BITE.

TOO STUFFED TO TAKE ANOTHER BITE.

TOO NEAR EXPLODING TO TAKE ANOTHER BITE.

THEN I GUESS YOU'RE TOO FULL FOR DESSERT.

NO, NO— DESSERTS I SWALLOW WHOLE.

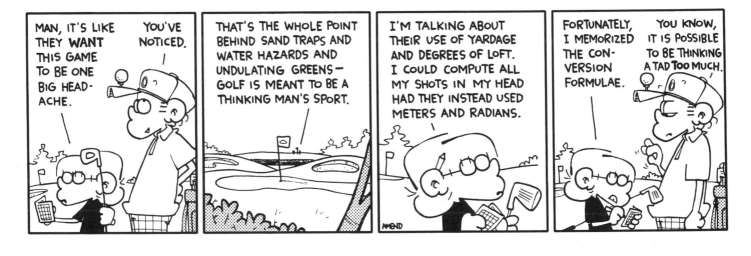

Panel 1:
WHAT'S THIS?

MY PROPOSED MENU FOR DINNER.

Panel 2:
I HAVE MY PHYSICS FINAL FIRST THING TOMORROW MORNING, SO I FIGURED I SHOULD PROBABLY EAT A REALLY GOOD MEAL TONIGHT.

Panel 3:
SORT OF LIKE THEY DO IN COMPETITIVE SPORTS?

I WAS THINKING MORE LIKE THEY DO ON DEATH ROW.

Panel 4:
YOU KNOW, IT'S FUNNY — I NEVER GOT THESE ULCER PAINS BACK WHEN I WAS TAKING EXAMS.

BY THE WAY, IN CASE I DIDN'T SPECIFY, THOSE SHOULD EACH BE TWO-POUND LOBSTERS.

Panel 5:
1. Compare and contrast Keats' "Ode to a Nightingale" with Byron's "Don Juan."

Panel 6:
4. Compare and contrast Blake's "Songs of Experience" with Wordsworth's "The Prelude."

Panel 7:
15. Compare and contrast Shelley's "Ode to the West Wind" with his earlier "Ozymandias."

Panel 8:
REMEMBER WHEN YOU READ US THAT ONE POEM THAT SAID THAT "LESS IS MORE"?

I SEE YOU AT LEAST ANSWERED THE QUESTIONS LABELED "YOUR NAME" AND "TODAY'S DATE."

Panel 9:
I'M WORRIED ABOUT PAIGE.

OH?

Panel 10:
SHE'S BEEN SO STRESSED ABOUT FINAL EXAMS... SHE'S BEEN PULLING HER HAIR OUT ALL WEEK.

Panel 11:
SWEETHEART, RELAX. BEING STRESSED ABOUT FINALS IS PART OF BEING IN SCHOOL. HECK, I PULLED MY HAIR OUT ALL THE TIME AT HER AGE.

Panel 12:
WHY DO YOU THINK I'M WORRIED?

HMM. YOU MAY HAVE A POINT.

FoxTrot
by Bill Amend

FIGURES IT'S THE ONE LAUNCH WE TRY TO VIDEOTAPE THAT GOES COMPLETELY HAYWIRE.

SO WHICH LECTURE WILL YOUR MOM BE GIVING US FIRST?

66

69

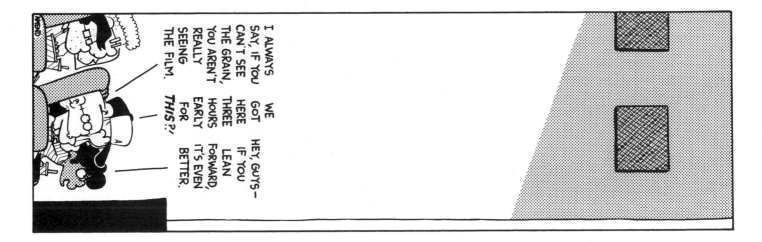

74

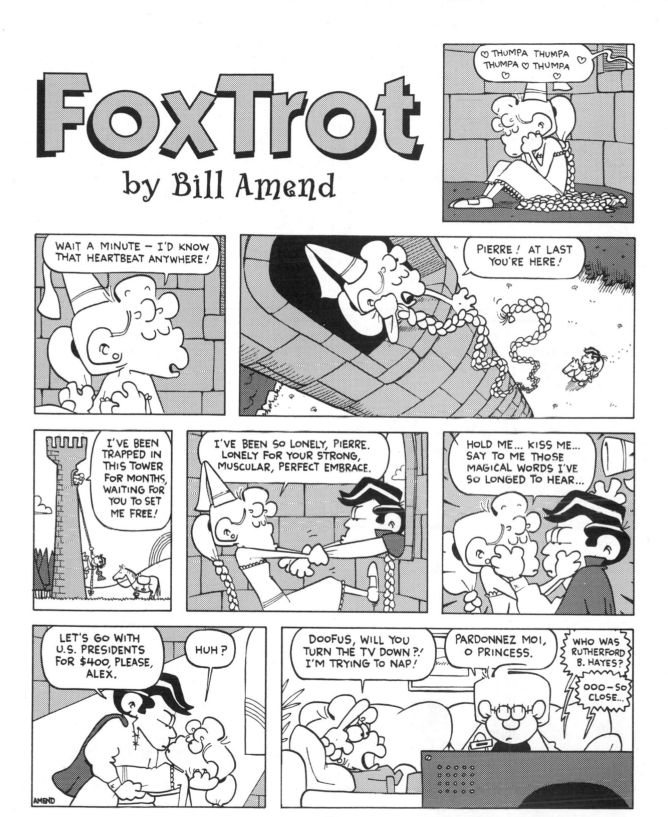

Panel 1:
(YAWN) GOOD MORNING, SWEETIE.
(YAWN) GOOD MORNING, DEAR.

Panel 2:
YOU'RE KISSING MY CHIN.
YOU'RE KISSING MY NOSE.

Panel 3:
NOW YOU'RE KISSING MY EYEBROWS.
NOW YOU'RE KISSING MY PILLOW.

Panel 4:
YOU KNOW, MAYBE WE SHOULD BE KEEPING SOME COFFEE IN THE BEDROOM.
ARE THESE YOUR LIPS HERE?

Panel 5:
ARRGH! STUPID MOSQUITOS!

Panel 6:
THEY'RE DRIVING ME NUTS!

Panel 7:
NO INSECT IS MORE ANNOYING IN MY BOOK!
SO WHY DON'T YOU GO INSIDE?

Panel 8:
JUST BECAUSE THERE AREN'T INSECTS MORE ANNOYING...
MY ELF WIZARD USES HIS SCROLL OF LOGIC.
AND THE PAIGE-TROLL'S HEAD EXPLODES! GOOD MOVE.

Panel 9:
PETER, COULD YOU PLEASE CARRY THAT TRASH BAG OUT TO THE CURB?
WHY'S IT ALWAYS ME, MOM?

Panel 10:
"PETER, TAKE THE TRASH OUT"... "PETER, TAKE THE RECYCLING OUT"... "PETER, TAKE MORE TRASH OUT"...

Panel 11:
COULDN'T YOU ASK JASON TO DO THIS SORT OF THING ONCE IN A WHILE?!

Panel 12:
WHAT MAKES YOU THINK I DON'T?
FIGURES IT'S EXTRA-HEAVY.

WELCOME TO THE INTERNET CHESS ZONE. PLEASE LOG IN.

GREETINGS, ROGER_FOX. THERE ARE CURRENTLY 1,526 OTHER PLAYERS ONLINE.

... 810 OTHER PLAYERS.
... 394 OTHER PLAYERS.
... 77 OTHER PLAYERS.
... 6 OTHER PLAYERS.

OK, SO I MIGHT HAVE MENTIONED YOU IN ONE OR TWO CHAT ROOMS.

WHAT'D YOU DO? TELL THEM HOW GOOD I AM?

TIMMY_AGE_3 SAYS, "LET'S RUMBLE."

ANDY, YOU'RE HITTING THE BALL THIN — KEEP YOUR HEAD DOWN.

LUCKY DUFY'S DRIVING RANGE

THIN AGAIN.

SWEETHEART, YOU ARE LIKE SUPER THIN... UNBELIEVABLY THIN... THINNER THAN THIN...

YO, MOM — SINCE WHEN DOES GOLF PUT YOU IN SUCH A GOOD MOOD?

SINCE I FIGURED OUT HOW TO PLAY IT.

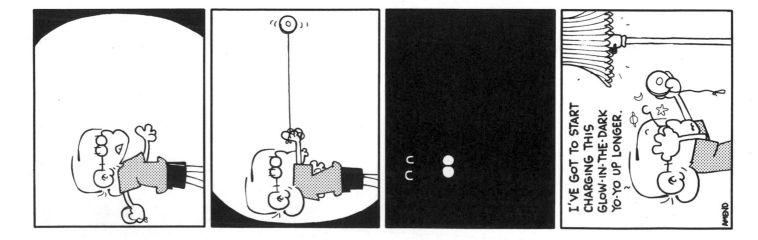

I'VE GOT TO START CHARGING THIS GLOW-IN-THE-DARK YO-YO UP LONGER.

90

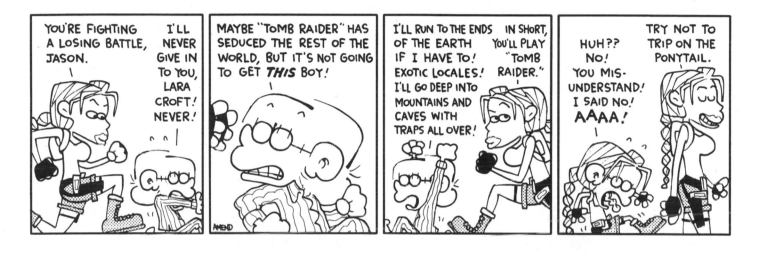

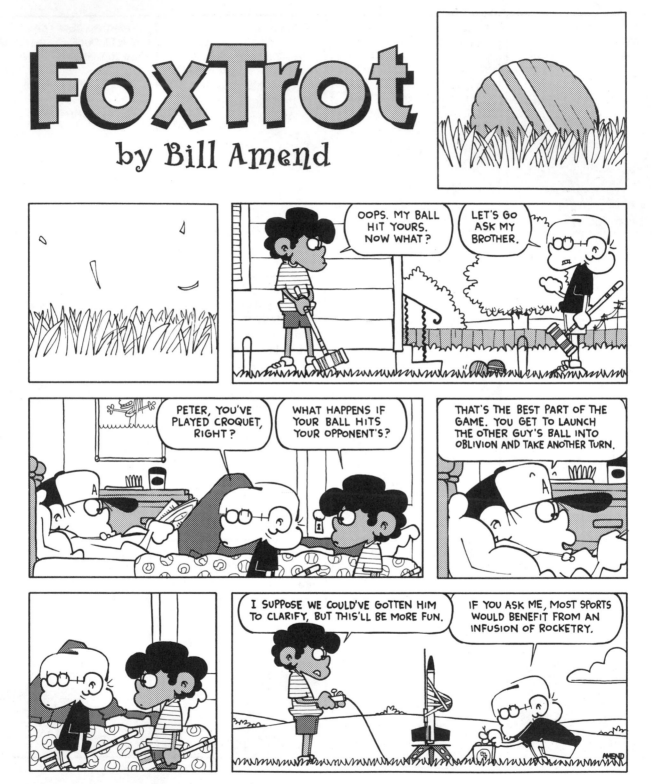

FoxTrot

by Bill Amend

HARD TO BELIEVE THERE WAS A TIME WHEN I LOOKED FORWARD TO THREE-DAY WEEKENDS.

JASON, WILL YOU COOL IT WITH THE PACING?!

A PERFECTLY GOOD MONDAY WITHOUT SCHOOL! HOW CAN YOU STAND IT?!

WHAT ARE THOSE?

CARPET SAMPLES. I'M THINKING ABOUT REDOING THE UPSTAIRS BEDROOMS.

THAT IVORY-COLORED STUFF WE HAVE NOW IS JUST A LITTLE TOO 1980s FOR MY TASTES.

IVORY? MY BEDROOM CARPET IS DARK GRAY.

ISN'T IT?

SPEAKING OF THE 1980s, WHEN WAS THE LAST TIME YOU VACUUMED IN THERE?

1. A class of 30 students is given a pop quiz.

If 12 of the students receive F's, what is the percentage of students who likely weren't paying attention during yesterday's lecture?

THIS TEACHER HAS A CRUEL STREAK I'M NOT SURE I LIKE.

I'M NOTICING ABOUT 40 PERCENT OF YOU SEEM STUCK ON PROBLEM ONE.

I SEE THE BACK-TO-SCHOOL VISA BILL CAME.

DO YOU REALIZE WE COULD SEND OUR KIDS NAKED TO HARVARD AND SAVE MONEY?

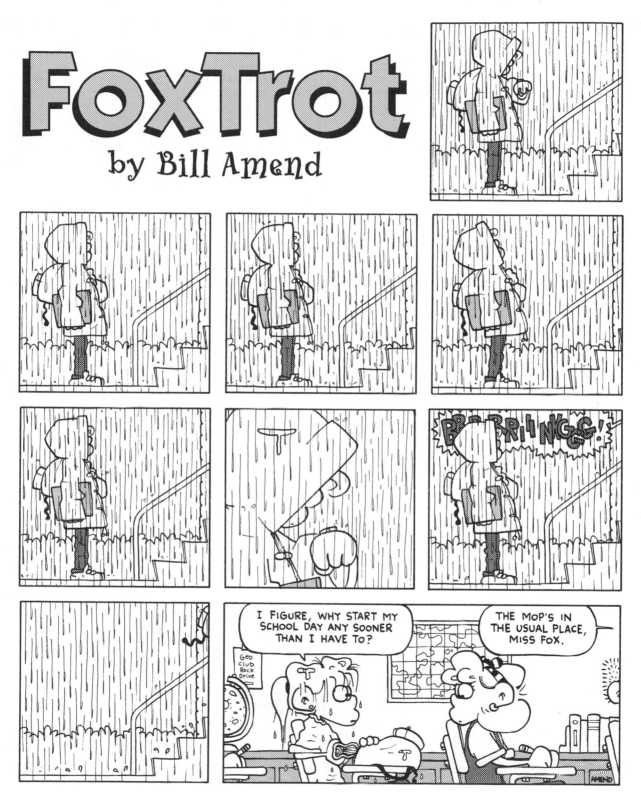

WOW. YOU KNOW, THIS "DILBERT" PHENOMENON IS AMAZING TO ME.

FIVE YEARS AGO I HADN'T EVEN HEARD OF THE COMIC STRIP, AND NOW IT'S EVERY-WHERE I LOOK. BOOKS... CALENDARS...OFFICE SUPPLY ADS... HIS OWN ICE CREAM FLAVOR... NOW I READ ABOUT AN UPCOMING TV SERIES...

WHATEVER SCOTT ADAMS' SECRET FORMULA IS, IT SURE HAS BEEN SUCCESSFUL.

I'M A LITTLE SURPRISED OTHER CARTOONISTS HAVEN'T TRIED TO COPY IT.

HONEY, PLEASE. THESE ARE ARTISTS. THEY HAVE INTEGRITY.

SO, LIKE MY NEW HAIR-CUT?

APPARENTLY "DILBERT'S" BIG LEAP FROM OBSCURITY TO PROMINENCE BEGAN SOON AFTER SCOTT ADAMS STARTED INCLUDING HIS INTERNET ADDRESS BETWEEN THE PANELS OF HIS STRIP, BEFORE SUCH THINGS WERE COMMON.

NOW THAT EVERYONE IS DOING IT, I WONDER WHAT A CARTOONIST COULD DO TO DISTINGUISH HIMSELF FROM THE PACK.

**www.
foxtrot
.com**

...WITHOUT LOOKING TOO DESPERATE.

I'M SURE IT'S ALL PART OF THE CREATIVE CHALLENGE.

I SUSPECT ANOTHER THING THAT'S REALLY HELPED "DILBERT" SUCCEED COMMER-CIALLY IS ITS THREE-PANEL FORMAT.

HOW IS THAT AN ADVAN-TAGE?

SO MANY OF THE OTHER STRIPS I SEE ARE FOUR PANELS. THAT MEANS SCOTT ADAMS GETS AN INSTANT 33-PERCENT PRODUCTIVITY JUMP ON HIS COMPETITORS. THIS IS PROBABLY HOW HE HAS THE TIME FOR ALL THOSE LUCRATIVE SIDE PROJECTS.

I'LL BET ANY FOUR-PANEL CARTOONISTS REALIZING THIS MUST BE BEATING THEIR HEADS ON THEIR DESKS RIGHT ABOUT NOW.

NNOOTT LLIITTEERRAALLLLYY, OOFF CCOOUURRSSEE.

110

Panel 1: ANOTHER CLEVER THING SCOTT ADAMS DID EARLY ON WAS TO ESTABLISH AN ELECTRONIC NEWSLETTER FOR FANS.

MOM, I'M OFF TO THE BOOKSTORE.

Panel 2: I IMAGINE THIS GIVES HIM QUITE A LEG UP ON THE COMPETITION, SINCE I'D WAGER CARTOONISTS DON'T HAVE MUCH P.R. MACHINERY AT THEIR DISPOSAL.

I HEAR THERE'S THIS GREAT NEW BOOK THAT'S JUST COME OUT.

Panel 3: THINK ABOUT IT— THE POWER TO INFORM AN ARMY OF FANS THE INSTANT YOU HAVE A NEW PRODUCT FOR SALE.

IT'S ONLY $12.95, TOO! A BARGAIN!

Panel 4: THE ONLY THING THAT COULD TOP THAT WOULD BE TO PLUG **THAT** STUFF IN THE STRIP ITSELF.

OH, COME ON— NO ONE COULD BE **THAT** SHAMELESS.

DID I MENTION THE ISBN NUMBER?

0-8362-

Panel 5: I THINK ONE OF THE THINGS "DILBERT's" SUCCESS REALLY DEMONSTRATES IS THE POWER OF NICHE APPEAL.

Panel 6: ORIGINALLY, THE STRIP WAS ABOUT ALL SORTS OF TOPICS. BUT ONCE SCOTT ADAMS REALIZED HE WAS STRIKING A CHORD WITH THE WORLD'S CUBICLE DWELLERS, HE FOCUSED ALMOST EXCLUSIVELY ON WORKPLACE HUMOR, AND SINCE THEN HE'S BECOME FILTHY RICH.

Panel 7: I GUESS THE LESSON FOR OTHER CARTOONISTS IS, IF YOU WANT TO MAKE IT BIG, FIND AN UNDERSERVED TARGET AUDIENCE AND GO AFTER IT.

Panel 8: RIGHT, KIDS?

NO, NO – I CALLED YOU "LASSIE."

MOM! JASON CALLED ME "HAGGIS FACE"!

Panel 9: NOW THAT I THINK ABOUT IT, MAYBE THE REASON CARTOONISTS AREN'T FLOCKING TO IMITATE "DILBERT" IS BECAUSE THEY **ARE** SMART.

Panel 10: MAYBE THEY RECOGNIZE THAT "DILBERT" IS SUCCESSFUL BECAUSE IT **IS** "DILBERT" — IT ISN'T TRYING TO FOLLOW SOMEONE ELSE'S FORMULA.

Panel 11: MAYBE THE KEY TO A GOOD COMIC STRIP IS TO FIND AND INCORPORATE IDEAS THAT OTHERS **AREN'T** CURRENTLY USING.

Panel 12: MOM! DAD! CHECK OUT THIS COOL STUFFED TIGER I FOUND!

PERHAPS I SHOULD INCLUDE THE RECENT PAST IN THERE AS WELL.

I DON'T KNOW. THERE'S SOMETHING TO BE SAID FOR NOSTALGIA.

FoxTrot
by Bill Amend

MOST PEOPLE JUST DON'T REALIZE THE INTERNET'S AWESOME POTENTIAL.

MIND IF I CHECK THE TRAFFIC AT MY MARCUS-CAM SITE?

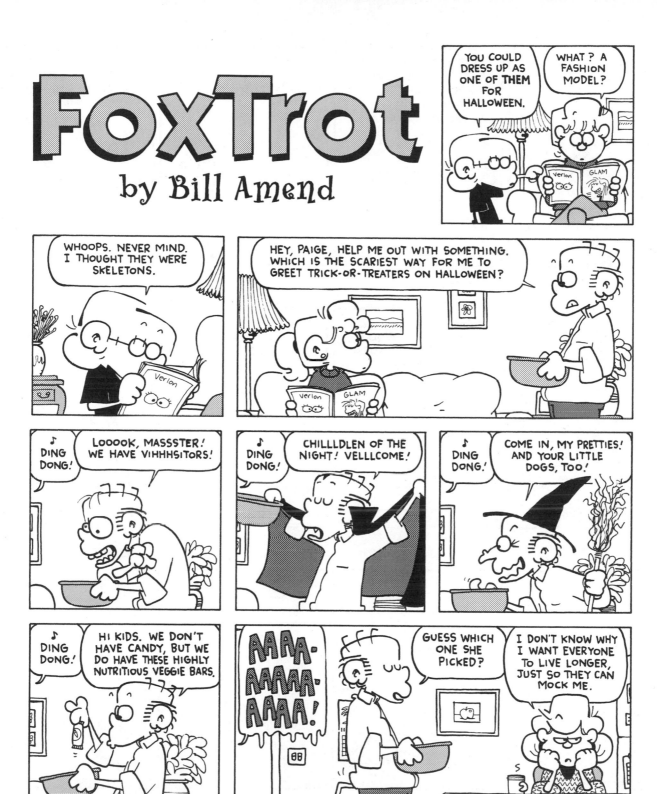

HOW GOES THE CLEAN-UP OF ALL YOUR LITTLE LEFT-OVER HALLOWEEN SURPRISES?

YOU'LL BE HAPPY TO KNOW THAT I'VE FINISHED WITH THE BASEMENT, GARAGE AND HALF OF THE LIVING ROOM.

AND YOU'RE GETTING EVERYTHING?

YUP. RUBBER HANDS, PLASTIC ZOMBIES, GLOW-IN-THE-DARK SKELETONS, SPRING-LOADED FLYING INTESTINES... ALL OF IT.

AND WHERE ARE YOU PUTTING IT ALL?

UM, THAT YOU'LL BE LESS HAPPY TO KNOW.

MOTH-ERRR!...

R.I.P.

WELL, THIS IS THE LAST OF IT.

YOU'RE SURE? I'M NOT GOING TO FIND ANY MORE OF THESE HALLOWEEN TRICKS OF YOURS HIDDEN SOMEWHERE?

NOPE. I SWEPT THE HOUSE TWICE. THIS LOAD OF RUBBER GHOULS FROM THE LINEN CLOSET IS THE LAST OF MY ARSENAL.

WHAT ABOUT ANY THINGS YOU MIGHT HAVE PLANTED OUTSIDE THE HOUSE?

NOW THAT YOU MENTION IT, THERE WAS THAT FAKE CORPSE I PUT IN DAD'S CAR.

WHERE? IN THE FRONT SEAT? THE BACK SEAT?

SIR, ARE YOU AWARE THAT THERE'S A SHOELACE DANGLING FROM YOUR TRUNK?

NO PROBLEM, OFFICER. LET'S OPEN IT UP AND FIND OUT WHY.

GHASTLY EYEBALLS PAINTED ON THE EGGS...

PLASTIC SPIDERS INSERTED INSIDE THE LOAF OF BREAD... STAGE BLOOD IN THE KNIFE DRAWER...

FAKE GREEN MOLD ALL OVER THE BACON STRIPS...

JASON, PROMISE ME NEXT YEAR YOU WON'T GO SO HALLOWEEN GOOFY.

WHAT WAS THAT PART ABOUT MOLD?

CRUNCH CRUNCH CRUNCH